THE FUNDAMENTALS OF ENGLISH GRAMMAR

Niketa Hrushikesh Joglekar

Title   :   The Fundamentals of English Grammar

Author   :   Niketa Hrushikesh Joglekar

Edition   :   First (September, 2024)

ISBN   :   9788197785726

Published by

PRACHI
DIGITAL PUBLICATION

Regd. Add.: 254, Khuriyakhatta No. 10, Bindukhatta,
Lalkuan, Nainital - 262402, Uttarakhand, India
Website : www.prachidigital.com
E-mail : info@prachidigital.in
Phone : +91 976041 7980, +91 976041 8103

Printed by :
Manipal Technologies Limited, Bengaluru - 560001, Karnataka

INDEX

CHAPTER 1

INTRODUCTION

1. Introduction

English grammar forms the cornerstone of effective communication. For students in grades 5-10, mastering the fundamentals of grammar is crucial for academic success and beyond. This book, "The Fundamentals of English Grammar for Grades 5-10," is designed to provide a comprehensive and accessible guide to the rules and conventions that govern the English language. It aims to equip young learners with the tools they need to express themselves clearly, confidently, and correctly. Understanding grammar is more than just knowing the rules of language; it's about understanding how language works. This book covers all essential aspects of English grammar, including parts of speech, sentence structure, punctuation, and usage.

It also delves into more complex areas such as clauses, phrases, and the intricacies of verb tenses. Each chapter is carefully structured to build on the previous one, ensuring a gradual and thorough understanding of the material. The journey begins with an exploration of the parts of speech. These are the building blocks of sentences and include nouns, pronouns, verbs, adjectives, adverbs, prepositions, conjunctions, and interjections. Understanding the function of each part of speech is essential for constructing meaningful and grammatically correct sentences. For instance, recognizing the difference between a noun and a pronoun can help students avoid common mistakes such as using "he" instead of "him" in a sentence. By mastering the parts of speech, students can begin to understand how words work together to convey meaning.

Next, the book delves into sentence structure, an area that often poses challenges for young learners. Sentences can be simple, compound, or complex, and each type serves a different purpose in writing. A simple sentence contains one independent clause, while a compound sentence has two or more independent clauses joined by a conjunction. Complex sentences, on the other hand, contain an independent clause and one or more dependent clauses. Understanding these distinctions is crucial for effective writing. This book provides clear explanations and numerous examples to help students grasp these concepts. Punctuation is another critical area covered in this book. Proper punctuation is essential for clarity and meaning in writing. This book explains the use of periods, commas, semicolons, colons, question marks, exclamation points, quotation marks, and other punctuation marks.

Each mark serves a specific purpose, and incorrect usage can lead to confusion. For example, the misuse of a comma can change the meaning of a sentence entirely. By learning the correct use of punctuation, students can enhance the clarity and readability of their writing. Usage, or the correct way to use words in context, is another key focus of this book. English is full of words that are often confused, such as "their," "there," and "they're" or "affect" and "effect." Understanding the differences between these words and knowing when to use each one is essential for effective communication. This book provides detailed explanations and examples to help students avoid common usage errors. The book also addresses more advanced topics such as clauses and phrases.

Clauses are groups of words that contain a subject and a verb, and they can be independent or dependent. Phrases, on the other hand, are groups of words that work together but do not contain a subject and a verb. Understanding how to use clauses and phrases correctly can add variety and complexity to writing. This book provides clear explanations and examples to help students master these concepts. Verb tenses are another important aspect of English grammar covered in this book. English has twelve tenses, each of which serves a different purpose. The book explains the use of each tense and provides examples to help students understand how to use them correctly. For instance, the present perfect tense is used to describe actions that occurred at an unspecified time in the past, while the past continuous tense is used to describe actions that were ongoing at a specific time in the past. By mastering verb tenses, students can express themselves more accurately and effectively.

This book also includes numerous exercises and activities to reinforce learning. Each chapter contains practice exercises designed to help students apply what they have learned. These exercises range from simple fill-in-the-blank questions to more complex writing assignments. By completing these exercises, students can gain a deeper understanding of the material and develop their grammar skills. In addition to practice exercises, this book also includes review sections at the end of each chapter. These reviews summarize the key points covered in the chapter and provide additional practice questions. This helps students review and reinforce their learning and ensures they have a solid understanding of the material before moving on to the next chapter. Furthermore, this book recognizes the importance of engaging students in the learning process. It includes fun and interactive activities such as games, puzzles, and group projects. These activities make learning grammar enjoyable and help students develop a positive attitude toward the subject.

For example, a grammar scavenger hunt can be a fun way for students to review parts of speech, while a group project can help them practice constructing complex sentences. This book also includes tips and strategies for effective writing. Good writing is not just about correct grammar; it's also about clarity, coherence, and style. This book provides guidance on how to organize ideas, develop a clear thesis statement, and use transitions effectively. It also includes tips on how to vary sentence structure and word choice to make writing more interesting and engaging. Finally, this book recognizes that every student learns differently. It includes a variety of teaching approaches and techniques to accommodate different learning styles.

For example, visual learners may benefit from diagrams and charts, while auditory learners may benefit from listening to explanations and discussions. By providing a range of learning tools and resources, this book ensures that all students can succeed in learning grammar. The Fundamentals of English Grammar for Grades 5-10 is a comprehensive and accessible guide to mastering English grammar. It covers all essential aspects of grammar, from parts of speech and sentence structure to punctuation and usage. It also addresses more advanced topics such as clauses, phrases, and verb tenses. With clear explanations, numerous examples, and engaging exercises and activities, this book provides students with the tools they need to succeed in writing and communication.

Whether you are a student, teacher, or parent, this book is an invaluable resource for learning and teaching grammar.

1.1. Purpose of the Book

The primary purpose of "The Fundamentals of English Grammar for Grades 5-10" is to serve as an essential resource for students, teachers, and parents, ensuring that middle and high school learners acquire a robust understanding of English grammar. This comprehensive guide is meticulously crafted to address several key objectives that are critical for students' academic and personal growth. First and foremost, the book aims to enhance students' communication skills. In an increasingly globalized world, clear and effective communication is paramount. Mastering the rules and conventions of English grammar enables students to express their ideas more precisely and persuasively, which is vital not only in academic settings but also in everyday interactions and future professional endeavors. By providing detailed explanations and practical examples, the book helps students improve both their written and spoken English, fostering their ability to convey thoughts and ideas coherently and confidently. Another significant purpose of this book is to build academic success.

Proficiency in grammar is a cornerstone of academic achievement, impacting performance across all subjects. Strong grammar skills contribute to better writing, clearer presentations, and more accurate understanding of complex texts. This book equips students with the grammatical tools necessary to excel in their studies, from crafting essays and reports to tackling standardized tests and college entrance exams. By ensuring a solid foundation in grammar, the book lays the groundwork for students to achieve academic excellence and reach their full potential. Moreover, "The Fundamentals of English Grammar for Grades 5-10" aims to develop critical thinking skills. Understanding and applying grammatical rules requires analytical thinking and a deep understanding of how language works. This book encourages students to engage with language on a deeper level, analyzing sentence structures, identifying parts of speech, and recognizing the nuances of word usage.

Through this process, students not only become proficient in grammar but also enhance their overall cognitive abilities, fostering a more profound appreciation for the intricacies of the English language. Promoting language proficiency is another core objective of this book. Language proficiency encompasses a comprehensive understanding of syntax, semantics, and usage, going beyond basic communication skills. By covering all essential aspects of grammar, from parts of speech and sentence structure to punctuation and verb tenses, the book elevates students' command of the English language. Detailed explanations, numerous examples, and practice exercises ensure that students gain a thorough understanding of grammatical concepts, enabling them to use language with precision and confidence. Furthermore, this book seeks to foster confidence in writing.

Many students struggle with writing due to a lack of confidence in their grammar skills. "The Fundamentals of English Grammar for Grades 5-10" addresses this issue by offering clear, straightforward explanations of grammatical rules, accompanied by practical exercises that reinforce learning. By mastering the fundamentals of grammar, students can approach writing tasks with greater assurance and competence, leading to improved writing skills and a more positive attitude toward writing. Encouraging lifelong learning is another important purpose of this book. Grammar is not just a subject to be learned in school; it is a lifelong skill that enhances personal and professional communication. This book aims to instill a love of learning and a curiosity about language that students will carry with them beyond the classroom. By understanding the importance of grammar and its applications in various contexts, students are encouraged to continue refining and developing their language skills throughout their lives.

In addition to benefiting students, this book serves as a valuable resource for teachers and parents. Educators can use the book as a structured guide to teaching grammar, complete with lesson plans, exercises, and activities that align with curriculum standards. Parents can also use the book to support their children's learning at home, assisting with homework and reinforcing classroom instruction. By providing clear and accessible explanations of grammatical concepts, the book empowers teachers and parents to effectively support students' language development. Addressing common challenges and mistakes is another key objective of this book. Many students face similar difficulties when learning grammar, such as confusing homophones or misplacing punctuation marks. "The Fundamentals of English Grammar for Grades 5-10" tackles these issues head-on, offering strategies and tips for avoiding and correcting errors.

By identifying common pitfalls and providing targeted practice, the book helps students overcome obstacles and improve their grammar skills more effectively. The book also aims to incorporate engaging and interactive learning methods. Traditional grammar instruction can sometimes be perceived as dry and unengaging, leading to a lack of interest and motivation among students. To counter this, the book includes interactive activities, games, and puzzles that make learning grammar enjoyable and memorable. These methods not only enhance students' understanding of grammatical concepts but also foster a positive and enthusiastic attitude toward learning. Supporting diverse learning styles is another essential purpose of this book. Every student learns differently, and the book is designed to accommodate a variety of learning preferences.

It includes visual aids such as charts and diagrams, auditory components such as explanations and discussions, and kinesthetic activities that involve movement and hands-on practice. By addressing different learning styles, the book ensures that all students have the opportunity to succeed in mastering grammar. Preparing students for future academic and career success is also a central objective of this book. Proficiency in grammar is a crucial skill for future endeavors, whether students are writing college application essays, creating resumes, or communicating in a professional setting. "The Fundamentals of English Grammar for Grades 5-10" provides students with a thorough grounding in grammar, equipping them with the skills they need to navigate future challenges and opportunities with confidence and competence. Encouraging independent learning is another key aim of this book. It includes self-assessment tools, review sections, and practice exercises that promote autonomy and self-motivation.

By fostering a sense of responsibility for their learning, the book helps students develop the skills they need to become lifelong learners, capable of independently acquiring and applying knowledge. Finally, the book aims to create a positive and supportive learning environment. It emphasizes the importance of patience, practice, and perseverance in mastering grammar. By providing clear guidance, constructive feedback, and ample opportunities for practice, the book encourages students to approach grammar with a growth mindset, understanding that mistakes are part of the learning process and that improvement comes with effort and persistence. In summary, the purpose of "The Fundamentals of English Grammar for Grades 5-10" is to provide a comprehensive, engaging, and accessible resource for mastering English grammar. By enhancing communication skills, building academic success, developing critical thinking, promoting language proficiency, fostering confidence in writing, encouraging lifelong learning, supporting teachers and parents, addressing common challenges, incorporating interactive learning methods, supporting diverse learning styles, preparing for future success, encouraging independent learning, and creating a positive learning environment, this book aims to equip students with the tools they need to excel in their studies and beyond. It is a valuable resource for students, teachers, and parents alike, dedicated to promoting a deep and lasting understanding of English grammar.

1.2. How to Use This Book

To maximize the benefits of "The Fundamentals of English Grammar for Grades 5-10," it is essential to approach the book with a structured and systematic method. The book is designed to build a comprehensive understanding of grammar through a logical progression of topics, starting from basic concepts and moving to more advanced ones. Begin by reviewing the table of contents to get an overview of the material and the sequence in which topics are presented. This will help you identify the key areas of focus and understand the flow of the book. Students should start each chapter by carefully reading the introductory explanations and definitions. The book provides numerous examples to illustrate how grammatical rules are applied in real-world contexts, making abstract concepts more tangible and easier to grasp. After reading the explanations, it is crucial to complete the practice exercises at the end of each section. These exercises are designed to reinforce learning and provide immediate feedback on comprehension. Approach these exercises with diligence and honesty, as they are integral to the learning process. Teachers can use this book as a primary or supplementary resource in their grammar instruction.

The clear explanations and structured format make it easy to integrate into lesson plans. Encourage students to engage actively with the material by asking questions and participating in discussions to deepen their understanding. Incorporate group activities and collaborative exercises to make learning more interactive and enjoyable. For instance, sentence construction games or peer review sessions can enhance students' grasp of grammar in a fun and engaging manner. Parents can support their children's learning by reviewing the material together and helping with practice exercises. This book provides an excellent opportunity for parents to be involved in their children's education, offering guidance and encouragement as needed. Create a quiet, distraction-free environment for study sessions to ensure that children have the focus and concentration required to absorb the material effectively. Regularly reviewing completed exercises and discussing any mistakes or misunderstandings can also help solidify learning.

The book includes review sections and self-assessment tools at the end of each chapter. Students should use these resources to evaluate their understanding and identify areas where they may need additional practice. These reviews help consolidate learning and ensure that students are prepared to move on to more complex topics. Set personal goals and timelines for completing each chapter, and use the exercises and review sections to monitor progress. Revisiting challenging concepts and practicing regularly are key to achieving mastery. Interactive activities, such as games and puzzles, are included to make learning more engaging. Students should take advantage of these activities to break up the monotony of traditional study methods and reinforce their understanding in a fun and memorable way. Visual aids, such as charts and diagrams, are also provided to support different learning styles.

Use these visual tools to help visualize complex grammatical structures and relationships, making them easier to understand and remember. For independent learners, the book offers a self-paced study guide. Set personal goals and timelines for completing each chapter, using the exercises and review sections to monitor progress. Revisiting challenging concepts and practicing regularly will help solidify understanding and promote long-term retention. The book encourages a growth mindset, reminding students that learning grammar is a gradual process requiring patience and perseverance. In summary, "The Fundamentals of English Grammar for Grades 5-10" is a versatile and comprehensive resource for learning and teaching grammar. By following the structured progression of the book, actively engaging with the material, completing practice exercises, utilizing review sections, and incorporating interactive activities, students can develop a strong foundation in English grammar.

Teachers and parents play a crucial role in guiding and supporting students through this process, creating an environment conducive to learning and encouraging a positive attitude toward grammar. Through consistent effort and practice, students will gain the skills and confidence needed to excel in their academic and personal communication.

1.3. Importance of Grammar

The importance of grammar in the context of "The Fundamentals of English Grammar for Grades 5-10" cannot be overstated. Grammar is the structural foundation of our ability to express ourselves. The rules of grammar help govern the sounds, words, sentences, and other elements, as well as their combination and interpretation, within a language. For students in grades 5-10, mastering grammar is particularly critical, as it lays the groundwork for effective communication, academic success, and cognitive development, extending its benefits well into their personal and professional lives.

- Firstly, grammar is essential for clear communication. It provides the structure needed to convey messages accurately and effectively. Without a proper understanding of grammar, our language would be disorganized and confusing, making it difficult to understand one another. For middle and high school students, this clarity is crucial as they begin to engage in more complex forms of communication. Whether writing essays, reports, or even participating in class discussions, a solid grasp of grammar allows students to articulate their thoughts clearly and persuasively. This clarity not only aids in getting their point across but also helps in building confidence in their ability to communicate effectively.

- Moreover, a strong foundation in grammar is closely linked to academic success. Proficiency in grammar enhances students' reading and writing skills, which are fundamental across all subjects. In subjects like history or science, for instance, students are often required to write detailed explanations, reports, and analyses. A good command of grammar enables them to construct well-organized and coherent arguments, which are essential for scoring well on assignments and exams. Furthermore, standardized tests, which play a significant role in academic assessment and college admissions, often include sections on grammar and writing. By mastering the fundamentals of grammar, students can improve their performance on these tests, thereby enhancing their overall academic prospects.

- Grammar also plays a vital role in cognitive development. Understanding and applying grammatical rules require analytical thinking and problem-solving skills. When students learn grammar, they are essentially learning how to think critically about language and its structure. This process involves recognizing patterns, making distinctions between different types of words and phrases, and understanding how these elements work together to create meaning. Such analytical skills are transferable to other areas of learning and life, fostering a more systematic and logical approach to problem-solving.

- Additionally, grammar proficiency contributes significantly to reading comprehension. As students progress through their education, the complexity of the texts they encounter increases. A good grasp of grammar helps students parse these texts more effectively, allowing them to understand and interpret nuanced meanings, infer context, and draw connections between ideas. This deeper level of comprehension is crucial for engaging with complex literature and academic texts, enabling students to extract and synthesize information more effectively.

- In the context of writing, grammar is indispensable for producing polished and professional work. Errors in grammar can distract from the content of the writing, undermine the writer's credibility, and impede the reader's understanding. For students, producing grammatically correct work is essential for achieving high grades and positive feedback. Beyond school, these skills are equally important in higher education and professional settings, where clear and error-free communication is often a prerequisite for success. Whether drafting a college application essay, crafting a business proposal, or writing a research paper, strong grammar skills are essential.

- Furthermore, grammar is a crucial component of effective language learning. For students learning English as a second language, grammar provides the framework needed to understand and use the language correctly. It helps them build sentences that are not only accurate but also natural-sounding. A strong grasp of English grammar also facilitates the learning of other languages, as many grammatical concepts are universal or have parallels in other linguistic systems.

- In addition to these practical benefits, studying grammar enhances students' appreciation of language and its intricacies. Language is one of the most powerful tools we have for expressing our identity, emotions, and thoughts.

By understanding its structure and rules, students can gain a deeper appreciation for the beauty and complexity of language. This appreciation can foster a lifelong interest in reading, writing, and learning, enriching their intellectual and cultural lives.

- Moreover, grammar instruction supports the development of soft skills, such as attention to detail, patience, and perseverance. Learning grammar requires careful attention to detail and the ability to recognize and correct mistakes. This meticulousness is a valuable skill in many areas of life, from academic research to professional work. Additionally, the process of learning grammar, with its rules and exceptions, fosters patience and perseverance. Students learn that mastery takes time and practice, teaching them the value of persistence and dedication.

- The importance of grammar also extends to digital communication, which has become increasingly prevalent in students' lives. Whether texting, emailing, or posting on social media, the ability to write clearly and correctly is essential. While digital communication often involves more informal language, a good understanding of grammar helps students adapt their writing to different contexts and audiences, ensuring that their messages are understood and taken seriously.

In conclusion, the importance of grammar in "The Fundamentals of English Grammar for Grades 5-10" is multifaceted and far-reaching. It is essential for clear and effective communication, academic success, cognitive development, reading comprehension, and professional writing. Additionally, it supports language learning, enhances appreciation of language, and fosters the development of valuable soft skills. By providing students with a solid foundation in grammar, this book equips them with the tools they need to succeed in their academic pursuits and beyond, helping them become confident, articulate, and competent communicators. The benefits of mastering grammar extend well beyond the classroom, influencing every aspect of students' personal and professional lives.

CHAPTER- 2

THE SENTENCES

2. The Sentence

Understanding sentences is fundamental to effective communication and writing. A sentence is a coherent group of words that conveys a complete thought and typically includes a subject and a predicate. It serves as the building block of written and spoken language, enabling us to express ideas clearly and comprehensively. At its core, a sentence must have two essential components: a subject and a predicate. The subject of a sentence is the person, place, thing, or idea that the sentence is about. It can be a single word or a complex noun phrase. For example, in the sentence "The cat slept on the couch," "The cat" is the subject. The predicate, on the other hand, contains the verb and provides information about what the subject is doing or what is happening to it. In the same example, "slept on the couch" is the predicate, describing the action of the subject. Sentences can be classified into different types based on their structure and function. Simple sentences contain a single independent clause, which expresses a complete thought. For instance, "She reads every day" is a simple sentence with a straightforward subject-predicate structure. Compound sentences combine two or more independent clauses using coordinating conjunctions like "and," "but," or "or."

An example is "I wanted to go to the beach, but it started raining." Here, two independent clauses are joined by the conjunction "but." Complex sentences include one independent clause and at least one dependent clause. The dependent clause provides additional information and cannot stand alone as a complete sentence. For example, "Although it was raining, we decided to go hiking" features a dependent clause ("Although it was raining") and an independent clause ("we decided to go hiking"). This structure allows for more detailed and nuanced expressions of ideas. Compound-complex sentences incorporate elements of both compound and complex sentences. They contain at least two independent clauses and one or more dependent clauses. An example is "She was late because she missed the bus, but she still managed to catch the end of the movie." This sentence combines two independent clauses with a dependent clause, creating a more elaborate structure. Sentences also vary in length and complexity, ranging from brief and straightforward to long and intricate. Short sentences are often used for emphasis or clarity, while longer sentences can provide detailed descriptions or elaborate on complex ideas.

However, overuse of lengthy sentences can lead to confusion or loss of clarity, so it's important to balance sentence length and structure for effective communication. Furthermore, sentence fragments—incomplete sentences that lack a subject or a predicate—can disrupt the flow of writing. For example, "Because I was tired" is a fragment that needs completion to form a full thought, such as "Because I was tired, I went to bed early." Properly structured sentences ensure that ideas are conveyed clearly and comprehensively. In summary, sentences are the fundamental units of written and spoken language, essential for expressing complete thoughts. By understanding and utilizing different sentence types and structures, such as simple, compound, complex, and compound-complex sentences, one can enhance the clarity and effectiveness of communication. Balancing sentence length and structure, while avoiding fragments and ensuring coherence, contributes to successful writing and effective expression.

2.1. Definition and Types of Sentences

The chapter categorizes sentences into four main types based on their purpose: declarative, interrogative, imperative, and exclamatory. Declarative sentences make statements or express opinions and always end with a period. They are the most common type of sentence and are used to provide information or convey facts, such as "The sun sets in the west." Interrogative sentences, on the other hand, ask questions and end with a question mark. They are essential for seeking information and engaging in dialogue, exemplified by questions like "What time does the meeting start?" Imperative sentences give commands or make requests, often ending with a period but sometimes an exclamation mark for emphasis, such as "Please pass the salt."

Exclamatory sentences express strong emotions or excitement and always end with an exclamation mark, like "Wow, that's incredible!" Beyond these basic types, the chapter introduces more complex sentence structures, including compound and complex sentences. Compound sentences are formed by joining two or more independent clauses with coordinating conjunctions (such as "and," "but," or "or") or a semicolon. Each clause in a compound sentence can stand alone as a complete sentence, for example, "I wanted to go hiking, but it started to rain." This structure allows for connecting related ideas and creating more sophisticated sentences. Complex sentences contain one independent clause and one or more dependent clauses, with dependent clauses providing additional information but unable to stand alone. For instance, "Although it was raining, we decided to go hiking" includes the independent clause "we decided to go hiking" and the dependent clause "Although it was raining."

The chapter also covers compound-complex sentences, which combine elements of both compound and complex sentences. These sentences include at least two independent clauses and one or more dependent clauses, such as "Although it was raining, we went hiking, and we enjoyed the adventure." Mastering these various sentence structures helps students create more nuanced and detailed writing, enhancing their ability to express complex ideas and relationships. Additionally, the chapter addresses common errors such as sentence fragments and run-on sentences. Sentence fragments are incomplete sentences that lack either a subject or a predicate, leading to confusion and lack of clarity. For example, "Because I was late" is a fragment because it does not provide a complete thought. Run-on sentences occur when two independent clauses are improperly joined without proper punctuation or conjunctions, as in "I went to the store I forgot to buy milk." Understanding and correcting these errors is essential for clear and effective communication.

To reinforce these concepts, the chapter includes practical exercises and activities that encourage students to identify and construct different types of sentences. Exercises may involve categorizing sentences, correcting errors, or combining simple sentences into compound or complex forms. Visual aids, such as charts and diagrams, help students visualize sentence structures and understand their components. Interactive activities, like group discussions and peer reviews, provide opportunities for collaborative learning and application of the concepts. In summary, Chapter 1 of "The Fundamentals of English Grammar for Grades 5-10" lays a solid foundation for understanding sentences by defining their structure and exploring various types. By mastering declarative, interrogative, imperative, and exclamatory sentences, as well as more complex structures like compound and complex sentences, students build essential skills for effective communication. The chapter's focus on common errors and practical exercises ensures that students not only learn theoretical concepts but also apply them in their writing, paving the way for greater clarity and sophistication in their language use.

2.1.1 Definition of a Sentence

At its core, a sentence is a group of words that expresses a complete thought. It must contain at least two essential components: a subject and a predicate. The subject is the part of the sentence that tells us who or what the sentence is about, while the predicate explains what the subject is doing or provides information about the subject. This combination of subject and predicate forms a complete idea, making a sentence meaningful and coherent. For example, in the sentence "The cat sleeps," "The cat" is the subject and "sleeps" is the predicate.

Together, they convey a complete thought. Without either component, the group of words would be incomplete and would fail to function as a sentence.

2.1.2 Types of Sentences

Sentences can be categorized into different types based on their purpose and structure. Understanding these types is essential for effective communication, as each type serves a distinct function. The four main types of sentences are declarative, interrogative, imperative, and exclamatory.

1. Declarative Sentences

Declarative sentences make statements or express opinions. They are the most common type of sentence and are used to convey information. Declarative sentences always end with a period.

Examples:

- "The sun rises in the east."
- "She enjoys reading books."
- "This is a beautiful painting."

Declarative sentences are straightforward and are used extensively in both written and spoken language to share facts, describe events, and express thoughts or opinions.

2. Interrogative Sentences

Interrogative sentences ask questions. They are essential for obtaining information and engaging in dialogue. Interrogative sentences always end with a question mark.

Examples:

- "What time is it?"
- "Are you coming to the party?"
- "How do you solve this problem?"

These sentences are vital in everyday communication as they help gather information, clarify doubts, and facilitate conversations. Interrogative sentences can be further divided into yes/no questions, which expect a yes or no answer, and wh- questions, which begin with question words like who, what, where, when, why, and how.

3. Imperative Sentences

Imperative sentences give commands, make requests, or offer invitations. They are used to direct someone to do something. Imperative sentences can end with a period or an exclamation mark, depending on the tone.

Examples:

- "Please close the door."
- "Sit down."
- "Join us for dinner!"

Imperative sentences are direct and often imply the subject "you," even though it is not explicitly stated. They are common in instructions, commands, and requests.

4. Exclamatory Sentences

Exclamatory sentences express strong emotions or excitement. They convey feelings such as surprise, anger, happiness, or frustration and always end with an exclamation mark.

Examples:

- "What a beautiful day!"
- "I can't believe you did that!"
- "Wow, that's amazing!"

These sentences add emotional intensity to writing and speech, making them more expressive and engaging. However, they should be used sparingly to maintain their impact.

2.1.3 Complexities and Variations in Sentence Types

While the basic types of sentences are straightforward, sentences can also be complex and varied in their construction. This chapter introduces students to more advanced concepts, such as compound and complex sentences, which combine multiple clauses to convey more nuanced ideas.

1. Compound Sentences

Compound sentences consist of two or more independent clauses joined by a coordinating conjunction (such as "and," "but," or "or") or a semicolon. Each clause in a compound sentence can stand alone as a complete sentence.

Examples:

- "I wanted to go for a walk, but it started to rain."
- "She loves reading books, and he enjoys watching movies."
- "You can have tea, or you can have coffee."

Compound sentences are useful for connecting related ideas and adding variety to writing. They help create more sophisticated and engaging sentences.

2. Complex Sentences

Complex sentences contain one independent clause and one or more dependent clauses. A dependent clause, also known as a subordinate clause, cannot stand alone as a complete sentence and relies on the independent clause for meaning.

Examples:

- "Although it was raining, we decided to go for a walk."
- "She finished her homework before she went out to play."
- "When the bell rang, the students quickly gathered their belongings."

Complex sentences allow writers to show relationships between ideas, such as cause and effect, contrast, or time. They add depth and detail to writing, making it more informative and interesting.

3. Compound-Complex Sentences

Compound-complex sentences combine elements of both

compound and complex sentences. They contain at least two independent clauses and one or more dependent clauses.

Examples:

- "Although it was late, we decided to watch another movie, and we ended up staying up all night."
- "She didn't like the cake, but she ate it anyway because she was hungry."
- "The teacher returned the homework after she noticed the error, but she asked the student to correct it."

These sentences are the most sophisticated type of sentence structure, allowing for the expression of multiple ideas and relationships within a single sentence. Mastering compound-complex sentences enables students to write with greater complexity and nuance.

2.1.4 Practical Applications and Exercises

To reinforce the concepts covered in this chapter, a variety of practical exercises and activities are included. These exercises range from identifying and constructing different types of sentences to correcting errors and combining clauses. By engaging in these activities, students can practice and apply what they have learned, gaining confidence in their ability to use sentences effectively. For instance, students might be given a list of sentences and asked to categorize them as declarative, interrogative, imperative, or exclamatory. They may also be tasked with rewriting simple sentences as compound or complex sentences, or combining multiple sentences into a compound-complex structure. These exercises not only reinforce the rules and structures discussed but also encourage students to think critically about sentence construction and its impact on communication.

2.1.5 Visual Aids and Interactive Components

To cater to different learning styles, the chapter includes visual aids such as charts and diagrams. These visual tools help students see the relationships between different parts of a sentence and understand how various sentence types are constructed. For example, a chart might break down a compound sentence into its independent clauses and show how they are joined by a conjunction. Interactive components, such as group activities and discussions, further enhance learning. Students might work in pairs or small groups to create sentences of different types or to identify and correct errors in sample sentences. These activities promote collaboration and peer learning, allowing students to share their insights and learn from one another.

Conclusion

This provides a thorough introduction to the definition and types of sentences. By understanding the basic structure of sentences and the different ways they can be used to convey information, ask questions, give commands, and express emotions, students lay the groundwork for effective communication.

Through a combination of explanations, examples, exercises, visual aids, and interactive activities, this chapter ensures that students gain a solid foundation in sentence construction. This knowledge is essential for mastering more advanced grammatical concepts and achieving success in both academic and personal communication.

2.2. Subject and Predicate

Understanding subjects and predicates is fundamental to

mastering English grammar, as they form the essential building blocks of sentence structure. Grasping the roles and nuances of these components is crucial for constructing coherent, meaningful sentences and effective communication. This comprehensive examination of subjects and predicates will explore their definitions, functions, types, and common issues, providing a detailed guide for students to better understand and apply these grammatical elements.

2.2.1 Definition and Function of the Subject

At its core, the subject of a sentence is the main element that indicates who or what the sentence is about. It is typically a noun or pronoun that performs the action of the verb or is described by the predicate. The subject provides the focus of the sentence, allowing the reader or listener to understand what the sentence is discussing. The subject answers the questions "Who?" or "What?" in relation to the action or state expressed in the predicate. The subject can be as simple as a single noun or pronoun. For instance, in the sentence "The dog barks," "The dog" is the subject, consisting of a definite article "The" and the singular noun "dog." This simple subject clearly identifies the entity performing the action. In contrast, subjects can also be more complex, involving additional descriptive words or phrases.

For example, in the sentence "The large, shaggy dog with a red collar barks loudly," the subject is expanded to "The large, shaggy dog with a red collar," providing more detail about the noun through adjectives and a prepositional phrase. Subjects can also be compound, meaning they consist of two or more nouns or pronouns joined by a conjunction. For example, in the sentence "The cat and the dog are playing," "The cat and the dog" is a compound subject, where both "The cat" and "The dog" share the action of the verb "are playing." This compound structure allows for the inclusion of multiple entities within a single subject, which can affect how the verb is used in the sentence. The predicate of a sentence is the part that provides information about the subject. It includes the verb and any additional words or phrases that complete the meaning of the verb. The predicate answers the questions "What is happening?" or "What is the subject doing or experiencing?"

by describing the action, state, or condition of the subject. A simple predicate may consist of just a verb. For example, in the sentence "She runs," "runs" is the predicate, indicating the action performed by the subject "She." However, predicates can be more complex, incorporating various elements such as objects, complements, and modifiers. For instance, in "She runs every morning at the park," the predicate "runs every morning at the park" includes the verb "runs," an adverbial phrase "every morning," and a prepositional phrase "at the park," which provide additional detail about the action.

2.2.2 Types of Objects and Complements

The predicate often includes objects, which are nouns or pronouns that receive the action of the verb. Objects can be categorized into direct and indirect. A direct object directly receives the action of the verb. For example, in "He reads a book," "a book" is the direct object receiving the action of "reads." An indirect object, on the other hand, is the recipient of the direct object and typically indicates to whom or for whom the action is performed. In "She gave him a gift," "him" is the indirect object, and "a gift" is the direct object. Predicates may also include complements, which are words or phrases that provide more information about the subject or object. Subject complements follow linking verbs and describe or identify the subject. For instance, in "She is a teacher," "a teacher" is a subject complement providing additional information about the subject "She." Object complements follow and modify the direct object, offering further detail. For example, in "They elected him president," "president" is an object complement that describes "him."

- **Combining Subject and Predicate**

A complete sentence is formed by combining a subject and a predicate. The subject provides the focus, while the predicate delivers the action or description related to that subject. For instance, in the sentence "The students completed their homework," "The students" is the subject, and "completed their homework" is the predicate. Together, they convey a complete thought, informing the reader about what the students did. The balance between subject and predicate is essential for sentence clarity and coherence. An effective sentence ensures that the subject and predicate work together harmoniously to convey a precise message. For example, "The teacher explained the lesson clearly" combines the subject "The teacher" with the predicate "explained the lesson clearly," providing a clear picture of what the teacher did and how.

- **Subject-Verb Agreement**

One of the key aspects of using subjects and predicates correctly is ensuring subject-verb agreement. This rule stipulates that the verb in the predicate must agree in number with the subject. A singular subject requires a singular verb, while a plural subject requires a plural verb. For example, "The cat sleeps" uses the singular verb "sleeps" to agree with the singular subject "The cat," while "The cats sleep" uses the plural verb "sleep" to match the plural subject "The cats." Subject-verb agreement extends beyond simple singular and plural forms to include more complex scenarios involving collective nouns, indefinite pronouns, and compound subjects. For instance, collective nouns such as "team" or "family" may take singular or plural verbs depending on whether the group is acting as a single unit or as individuals. Similarly, indefinite pronouns like "everyone" or "none" require careful consideration for correct verb agreement.

- **Complex Subjects and Predicates**

In more advanced sentence structures, the subject and predicate can become complex. Compound subjects or predicates involve multiple elements joined by conjunctions. For example, in "The cat and the dog are playing," the compound subject "The cat and the dog" is paired with the compound predicate "are playing," which describes the actions performed by both subjects. Complex sentences may also feature multiple clauses, each with its own subject and predicate. For example, in "The cat sleeps while the dog plays," there are two clauses: "The cat sleeps" and "the dog plays," each with its own subject and predicate. Managing these multiple components requires a good understanding of how subjects and predicates function within different clauses, ensuring that each clause is grammatically correct and contributes to the overall meaning of the sentence.

- **Common Errors with Subjects and Predicates**

Students often encounter common errors related to subjects and predicates. One frequent issue is mismatching subjects and verbs, such as "The dogs runs quickly" instead of "The dogs run quickly."

This error occurs when the verb does not agree with the subject in number, leading to grammatical inaccuracies. Another common problem is sentence fragments, where a subject or predicate is missing, resulting in incomplete thoughts. For example, "Although the cat" lacks a predicate and does not form a complete sentence.

Sentence fragments can be corrected by providing the missing component to complete the thought. Run-on sentences are another issue, occurring when two independent clauses are improperly joined without proper punctuation or conjunctions. For instance, "I went to the store I forgot to buy milk" is a run-on sentence. Correcting this involves using appropriate punctuation, such as a period or a comma with a conjunction, to separate the clauses.

- **Practical Application and Exercises**

To reinforce the understanding of subjects and predicates, students can engage in various practical exercises and activities. These might include identifying and categorizing different types of subjects and predicates, correcting errors in sample sentences, or constructing sentences with compound or complex structures. For instance, students could be given a list of sentences and asked to underline the subject and circle the predicate, helping them to visually distinguish between the two components. Another exercise might involve transforming simple sentences into compound or complex forms, allowing students to practice combining clauses and expanding their sentence structures. Interactive activities, such as group discussions or peer reviews, can further enhance learning by providing opportunities for collaborative exploration and feedback.

- **Visual Aids and Resources**

Visual aids, such as charts and diagrams, can be highly effective in teaching subjects and predicates. For example, a diagram might break down a sentence into its constituent parts, highlighting the subject and predicate and showing how they connect. This visual representation helps students understand the roles of each component and how they work together to form a complete sentence. Additionally, resources like grammar workbooks or online exercises can offer additional practice and reinforcement. These tools provide students with a variety of examples and activities to apply their knowledge of subjects and predicates, supporting their ongoing learning and development.

Conclusion

In conclusion, understanding subjects and predicates is fundamental to mastering English 1 grammar and constructing clear, coherent sentences. The subject identifies who or what the sentence is about, while the predicate provides information about the subject's actions or state.

Mastery of these components, including their complexities and common issues, is essential for effective communication and grammatical accuracy. Through detailed explanations, practical exercises, and visual aids, students can gain a comprehensive understanding of subjects and predicates, laying a solid foundation for further exploration of grammar and enhancing their overall writing and speaking skills.

CHAPTER - 3

PARTS OF SPEECH

3. Introduction of Speech

Parts of speech are essential components of language that define the roles of words within sentences, providing structure and meaning to communication. There are eight primary parts of speech, each with a distinct function. Nouns name people, places, things, or ideas, acting as subjects or objects in a sentence, such as "dog" in "The dog barked loudly." Pronouns replace nouns to avoid repetition and streamline sentences, like "she" in "Sarah said she would arrive soon." Verbs express actions, states, or occurrences, such as "runs" in "She runs every morning," indicating what the subject is doing. Adjectives describe or modify nouns and pronouns, answering questions like "What kind?" or "How many?" For example, "blue" in "The blue sky" provides additional detail about the noun "sky."

Adverbs modify verbs, adjectives, or other adverbs, often answering questions such as "How?" or "When?" For instance, "quickly" in "He speaks quickly" describes how the action is performed. Prepositions establish relationships between nouns or pronouns and other words in a sentence, indicating time, place, or direction, such as "under" in "The cat slept under the table." Conjunctions connect words, phrases, or clauses, facilitating more complex sentence structures.

Coordinating conjunctions like "and," "but," or "or" link equal elements, while subordinating conjunctions like "because" or "although" introduce dependent clauses, as seen in "I stayed home because it was raining." Interjections express strong emotions or reactions, often standing alone or inserted into sentences, such as "Wow!" or "Ouch!" These parts of speech work together to create coherent, meaningful sentences, enabling clear and effective communication. Understanding and mastering these components is crucial for constructing grammatically correct and contextually appropriate language.

3.1. Nouns: Types and Functions

Chapter 2 of "The Fundamentals of English Grammar for Grades 5-10" delves deeply into the world of nouns, focusing on their types and functions within sentences. Understanding nouns and their roles is crucial for mastering English grammar, as they are fundamental to sentence structure and meaning. This comprehensive exploration will cover the various types of nouns, their specific functions, and their importance in constructing clear and coherent sentences.

3.1.1 Types of Nouns

Nouns are categorized into several types based on their characteristics and the roles they play in sentences. The primary types of nouns include common nouns, proper nouns, collective nouns, abstract nouns, and compound nouns. Each type has distinct features and functions that contribute to the richness of language and the precision of expression.

- **Common Nouns**

Common nouns refer to general names of people, places, things, or ideas. They are not specific and do not capitalize unless they begin a sentence. Examples include "city," "dog," "teacher," and "happiness." Common nouns are essential for everyday communication because they name general categories and objects. For instance, in the sentence "The dog barked loudly," "dog" is a common noun referring to a general category of animal without specifying which dog.

- **Proper Nouns**

Proper nouns, in contrast, name specific people, places, organizations, or events and always begin with a capital letter. They distinguish particular individuals or entities from the general category. Examples include "John," "Paris," "Microsoft," and "Christmas." Proper nouns provide specificity and uniqueness. For instance, in "John visited Paris last summer," both "John" and "Paris" are proper nouns that identify specific people and places, respectively.

- **Collective Nouns**

Collective nouns refer to groups of individuals or things considered as a single unit. Examples include "team," "family," "flock," and "class." Despite referring to multiple entities, collective nouns are treated as singular when it comes to verb agreement. For example, in "The team is winning the game," "team" is a collective noun that denotes a group acting as one entity. Understanding collective nouns is important for ensuring correct verb agreement and maintaining grammatical consistency in sentences.

- **Abstract Nouns**

Abstract nouns denote ideas, concepts, or qualities that cannot be perceived with the senses. They represent intangible things like emotions, qualities, or conditions. Examples include "love," "freedom," "courage," and "wisdom."

In the sentence "Her courage inspired everyone," "courage" is an abstract noun representing a quality rather than a physical object. Abstract nouns are essential for discussing non-material aspects of human experience and thought.

- **Compound Nouns**

Compound nouns are formed by combining two or more words to create a single noun with a new meaning. They can be written as separate words, hyphenated, or as a single word. Examples include "toothbrush" (single word), "mother-in-law" (hyphenated), and "ice cream" (separate words). Compound nouns allow for the creation of specific terms that convey particular meanings, such as "ice cream" referring to a specific type of dessert. Understanding compound nouns helps in accurately expressing complex ideas and objects.

3.1.2 Functions of Nouns

Nouns perform several key functions in sentences, each contributing to the structure and meaning of the sentence. The primary functions include serving as subjects, objects, and complements.

- **Subjects**

As subjects, nouns indicate who or what is performing the action of the verb or being described in the sentence. They are essential for identifying the main focus of the sentence. For instance, in the sentence "The teacher explained the lesson," "The teacher" is the subject noun that performs the action of "explained." The subject noun establishes the entity responsible for the action and provides context for the rest of the sentence.

- **Objects**

Nouns can also function as objects in a sentence. There are two main types of objects: direct objects and indirect objects.

1. **Direct Objects**: A direct object receives the action of the verb directly. For example, in "She read the book," "the book" is the direct

object noun receiving the action of "read." Direct objects are crucial for completing the meaning of the verb and providing additional detail about what is affected by the action.

2. **Indirect Objects**: An indirect object denotes to whom or for whom the action of the verb is performed. For instance, in "He gave his friend a gift," "his friend" is the indirect object noun indicating the recipient of the direct object "a gift." Indirect objects help to clarify the relationship between the action and its recipient.

- **Complements**

Nouns can also function as complements, providing additional information about other nouns or pronouns in the sentence. There are two main types of complements: subject complements and object complements.

1. Subject Complements: Subject complements follow linking verbs and provide more information about the subject. They often describe or identify the subject. For example, in "The winner is Jane," "Jane" is a subject complement that renames or identifies "The winner." Subject complements are essential for providing a complete understanding of the subject's identity or state.

2. Object Complements: Object complements follow and modify the direct object, offering further detail. For instance, in "They elected her president," "president" is an object complement that describes the direct object "her." Object complements enhance the meaning of the direct object by providing additional information about its role or status.

- **Noun Phrases**

Noun phrases are groups of words centered around a noun that function together as a single unit. A noun phrase typically includes the noun itself along with any adjectives, articles, or other modifiers that describe or limit the noun. For example, in "The old wooden chair in the corner," "The old wooden chair in the corner" is a noun phrase where "chair" is the main noun, and "the old wooden" and "in the corner" provide additional details. Noun phrases enrich the sentence by adding descriptive detail and specifying which noun is being referred to.

- **Possessive Nouns**

Possessive nouns show ownership or a relationship between entities. They are formed by adding an apostrophe and an "s" to a singular noun or just an apostrophe to a plural noun that is possessive.

For example, "Sarah's book" shows that the book belongs to Sarah, while "the teachers' lounge" indicates that the lounge belongs to multiple teachers. Possessive nouns are important for expressing relationships and ownership clearly and concisely.

- **Noun Usage in Different Contexts**

The usage of nouns can vary depending on the context and type of writing. For instance, in formal writing, such as academic essays or professional reports, nouns are used to convey precise and specific information. In contrast, in creative writing or storytelling, nouns may be used more evocatively to create vivid imagery and engage readers. Understanding the different contexts in which nouns are used helps in selecting the appropriate type and form of noun to achieve the desired effect.

- **Common Errors with Nouns**

Students often encounter several common errors with nouns, including issues with pluralization, possessive forms, and noun-verb agreement.

1. Pluralization Errors: Errors in pluralizing nouns can occur when adding "s" or "es" incorrectly or when dealing with irregular plurals. For example, "childs" instead of "children" is a common mistake. Ensuring correct plural forms is essential for grammatical accuracy.

2. Possessive Errors: Incorrect use of possessive forms, such as missing apostrophes or incorrect placement, can lead to confusion. For example, "its" versus "it's" can be challenging, where "its" indicates possession and "it's" is a contraction of "it is."

3. Noun-Verbs Agreement Errors: Misalignment between singular and plural nouns and verbs can disrupt sentence agreement. For instance, saying "The team are winning" instead of "The team is winning" is a frequent mistake that can affect clarity and grammatical correctness.

- **Practical Exercises and Activities**

To reinforce the understanding of nouns, students can engage in various practical exercises and activities. These might include identifying different types of nouns in sentences, creating sentences with specific types of nouns, and correcting errors related to nouns. For instance, students could be given sentences with missing nouns and asked to fill in the blanks with appropriate nouns.

- **Visual Aids and Resources**

Visual aids, such as charts and diagrams, can be effective in teaching about nouns. For example, a chart illustrating the different types of nouns and their examples can help students visualize and categorize nouns more effectively. Additionally, online resources and interactive grammar tools can provide additional practice and reinforcement, helping students apply their knowledge in various contexts.

Conclusion

In summary, Chapter 2 of "The Fundamentals of English Grammar for Grades 5-10" provides a comprehensive exploration of nouns, covering their types and functions in detail. By understanding common nouns, proper nouns, collective nouns, abstract nouns, and compound nouns, students can effectively identify and use nouns in various contexts. Mastery of noun functions, including subjects, objects, complements, and noun phrases, is essential for constructing clear and meaningful sentences. Practical exercises, visual aids, and resources further support students in applying their knowledge and improving their grammatical skills. Through this detailed examination of nouns, students gain a solid foundation for effective communication and enhanced writing proficiency.

3.2 Pronouns: Types and Usage

In the study of English grammar, understanding pronouns is essential for mastering sentence structure and achieving clarity in communication. Pronouns are words that replace nouns to avoid repetition and to streamline sentences, providing a more fluid and cohesive expression of ideas. This detailed exploration of pronouns will cover their various types, their functions within sentences, and the nuances of their usage.

3.2.1 Types of Pronouns

Pronouns are classified into several categories based on their roles and the relationships they express. The primary types of pronouns include personal pronouns, possessive pronouns, reflexive pronouns, intensive pronouns, demonstrative pronouns, relative pronouns, interrogative pronouns, and indefinite pronouns. Each type serves a specific purpose and is used in different contexts to replace nouns and convey meaning.

- **Personal Pronouns**

Personal pronouns refer to specific people or things and indicate the speaker, the listener, or others. They are categorized by person (first, second, and third) and number (singular or plural). The first-person pronouns, "I" and "we," refer to the speaker or speakers. For example, "I am going to the store" and "We are excited about the trip" use first-person pronouns to indicate the speaker or speakers. Second-person pronouns, "you," address the listener or readers, as in "You are invited to the party." Third-person pronouns, "he," "she," "it," "they," and their forms, refer to people or things other than the speaker and listener. For instance, "She enjoys reading" and "They are traveling to Europe" use third-person pronouns to talk about others.

- **Possessive Pronouns**

Possessive pronouns show ownership or possession. They replace nouns to indicate that something belongs to someone. The possessive pronouns include "my," "your," "his," "her," "its," "our," "their," and the corresponding possessive forms "mine," "yours," "hers," "ours," and "theirs." For example, in "This is my book," "my" indicates that the book belongs to the speaker. In "The book is hers," "hers" shows possession of the book without repeating the noun. Possessive pronouns are essential for expressing relationships and ownership clearly and concisely.

- **Reflexive Pronouns**

Reflexive pronouns are used when the subject and the object of the verb are the same person or thing. They end in "-self" or "-selves" and include "myself," "yourself," "himself," "herself," "itself," "ourselves," "yourselves," and "themselves." For example, in "She looked at herself in the mirror," "herself" reflects back to the subject "She," indicating that the action is directed at the same person. Reflexive pronouns are necessary for indicating that the subject performs an action on itself.

- **Intensive Pronouns**

Intensive pronouns, while similar in form to reflexive pronouns, are used to emphasize a noun or pronoun and do not function as the object of the verb. They include "myself," "yourself," "himself," "herself," "itself," "ourselves," "yourselves," and "themselves."

For example, in "The President himself attended the meeting," "himself" emphasizes the President's personal involvement. Intensive pronouns add emphasis and can highlight the importance of the subject or action.

- **Demonstrative Pronouns**

Demonstrative pronouns point to specific things or people and can indicate their relative position in space or time. The main demonstrative pronouns are "this," "that," "these," and "those." For instance, "This is my car" uses "this" to refer to something close to the speaker, while "Those are her shoes" uses "those" to refer to items that are farther away. Demonstrative pronouns are crucial for specifying and distinguishing particular items or people.

- **Relative Pronouns**

Relative pronouns introduce relative clauses and connect them to the main clause. They include "who," "whom," "whose," "which," and "that." For example, in "The book that she recommended was fascinating," "that" introduces the relative clause "that she recommended" and relates it to "the book." Relative pronouns are used to provide additional information about a noun and to create complex sentences by linking clauses.

- **Interrogative Pronouns**

Interrogative pronouns are used to ask questions and seek specific information. They include "who," "whom," "whose," "which," and "what." For instance, in "Who is coming to the party?" "who" is used to ask about the person attending the party. Interrogative pronouns help in formulating questions and obtaining details about people, objects, or situations.

- **Indefinite Pronouns**

Indefinite pronouns refer to non-specific people or things and do not point to particular entities. Examples include "anyone," "everyone," "someone," "nothing," "all," "some," and "few." For example, "Someone left their umbrella" uses "someone" to refer to an unspecified person. Indefinite pronouns are useful for discussing general concepts or unknown quantities and avoiding the repetition of nouns.

- **Usage and Agreement**

Correct usage of pronouns is essential for clarity and coherence in writing and speaking. Pronouns must agree with their antecedents in gender, number, and person. For example, if the antecedent is a singular, female person, the pronoun should be "she" or "her," not "he" or "his." In the sentence "The student lost her book," "her" agrees with the singular, female antecedent "student." Ensuring that pronouns and their antecedents match in gender and number prevents ambiguity and maintains grammatical accuracy.

- **Common Errors with Pronouns**

Several common errors can occur with pronouns, including issues with agreement, unclear antecedents, and incorrect usage.

1. Pronoun-Antecedent Agreement Errors: Errors can arise when pronouns do not agree with their antecedents in number or gender. For instance, "The team did their best" might be problematic if "team" is considered a singular unit, in which case "its best" would be correct.

2. Unclear Antecedents: Pronouns should have clear and unambiguous antecedents. For example, in "She told her friend that she would call her later," it may be unclear whether "she" refers to the same person or different individuals. Ensuring that pronouns clearly refer to their intended antecedents is crucial for clarity.

3. Incorrect Usage: Using the wrong type of pronoun or incorrectly placing intensive and reflexive pronouns can lead to confusion. For example, "Myself will handle the task" should be "I will handle the task" because "myself" is an intensive pronoun, not a subject pronoun.

- **Practical Exercises and Activities**

To reinforce understanding of pronouns, students can engage in various practical exercises and activities. These might include identifying and replacing nouns with appropriate pronouns, correcting sentences with pronoun errors, and creating sentences using different types of pronouns. For example, students could be given sentences with missing pronouns and asked to fill in the blanks with the correct pronoun based on context. Group discussions and peer reviews can also provide opportunities for collaborative learning and feedback.

- **Visual Aids and Resources**

Visual aids, such as charts and diagrams, can be helpful in teaching pronouns. A chart illustrating the different types of pronouns and their functions can aid in visualizing their roles and usage. Additionally, interactive grammar tools and online exercises can offer additional practice and support, helping students apply their knowledge in various contexts and reinforcing their understanding of pronouns.

Conclusion

In summary, understanding pronouns is fundamental to mastering English grammar and achieving clarity in communication. By recognizing and using different types of pronouns—personal, possessive, reflexive, intensive, demonstrative, relative, interrogative, and indefinite—students can effectively replace nouns, avoid repetition, and create coherent sentences. Proper usage and agreement of pronouns are crucial for grammatical accuracy and clarity, while practical exercises and visual aids further support learning and application. Through a thorough exploration of pronouns, students gain essential skills for effective writing and speaking, enhancing their overall proficiency in English grammar.

3.3 Verbs: Types and Tenses

In "The Fundamentals of English Grammar for Grades 5-10," the focus shifts to verbs, which are integral to sentence structure and meaning. Verbs are words that express actions, states, or occurrences and are crucial for constructing meaningful sentences. This section explores the different types of verbs and their tenses, providing a comprehensive understanding of how verbs function within the framework of English grammar.

3.3.1 Types of Verbs

Verbs can be categorized into several types based on their function and the roles they play in sentences. The primary types of verbs include action verbs, linking verbs, and auxiliary (helping) verbs. Each type serves a distinct purpose and contributes to the overall meaning of a sentence.

1. Action Verbs

Action verbs denote physical or mental actions performed by the subject of the sentence. They are dynamic and express activities or processes. Action verbs can be either transitive or intransitive.

- Transitive Verbs: These verbs require a direct object to complete their meaning. For example, in "She kicked the ball," "kicked" is a transitive verb, and "the ball" is the direct object receiving the action of the kick. Transitive verbs are essential for sentences where the action is directed towards something or someone.

- Intransitive Verbs: These verbs do not require a direct object to complete their meaning. For instance, in "He sleeps," "sleeps" is an intransitive verb with no direct object needed. Intransitive verbs can be used to describe actions that do not affect an external entity directly.

2. Linking Verbs

Linking verbs connect the subject of a sentence to a subject complement, which provides additional information about the subject. Unlike action verbs, linking verbs do not express actions but rather establish relationships between the subject and its complement. Common linking verbs include "be" (and its forms such as "am," "is," "are," "was," "were"), "seem," "become," and "appear."

For example, in "The cake smells delicious," "smells" is a linking verb connecting the subject "The cake" to the subject complement "delicious," which describes the cake's state.

3. Auxiliary Verbs

Auxiliary verbs, also known as helping verbs, are used in conjunction with main verbs to form different tenses, moods, and voices. The primary auxiliary verbs are "be," "have," and "do," and they assist in creating various verb forms.

- Be: The verb "be" is used to form continuous (progressive) tenses and passive voice. For example, "She is reading a book" uses "is" to form the present continuous tense, while "The book was written by her" uses "was" to form the passive voice.

- Have: The verb "have" is used to form perfect tenses. For instance, "They have finished their homework" uses "have" to create the present perfect tense, indicating that the action was completed at some point before now.

- Do: The verb "do" is used to form questions, negatives, and emphatic statements. For example, "Do you like ice cream?" uses "do" to form a question, while "She does not like ice cream" uses "does" to form a negative statement.

3.3.2 Tenses of Verbs

Tenses indicate the time of an action or state expressed by a verb. Understanding tenses is crucial for conveying when an action occurs, whether in the present, past, or future. The main tenses include the present, past, and future, each of which has simple, continuous (progressive), perfect, and perfect continuous forms.

1. Present Tense

The present tense describes actions or states occurring at the current time. It has four main forms:

- Simple Present: Used for habitual actions, general truths, or regular occurrences. For example, "She writes every day" indicates a routine action.

- Present Continuous (Progressive): Describes actions currently in progress. For instance, "He is studying right now" shows an ongoing activity.

- Present Perfect: Indicates actions that occurred at an unspecified time before now and have relevance to the present. For example, "They have traveled to many countries" suggests that their travels are significant to the present moment.

- Present Perfect Continuous: Describes actions that began in the past and are still continuing or have recently stopped. For instance, "She has been reading for two hours" indicates that she started reading in the past and continues to do so or has just finished.

2. Past Tense

The past tense describes actions or states that occurred at a specific time in the past. It includes the following forms:

- Simple Past: Used for actions that were completed at a definite time in the past. For example, "They visited the museum yesterday" indicates that the visit happened at a specific time.

- Past Continuous (Progressive): Describes actions that were ongoing at a particular time in the past. For instance, "She was cooking when the phone rang" shows an action in progress interrupted by another event.

- Past Perfect: Indicates actions that were completed before another point in the past. For example, "They had finished their meal before the guests arrived" shows that the meal was completed prior to the guests' arrival.

- Past Perfect Continuous: Describes actions that were ongoing in the past up to a specific point or until another action occurred. For instance, "He had been working at the company for ten years before he moved" indicates a continuous action that stopped before another past event.

3. Future Tense

The future tense describes actions or states that will occur after the present time. It has several forms:

- Simple Future: Used for actions that will happen at a future time. For example, "She will travel to Paris next month" indicates a planned future action.

- Future Continuous (Progressive): Describes actions that will be ongoing at a specific future time. For instance, "They will be meeting at noon" shows an action in progress at a future time.

- Future Perfect: Indicates actions that will be completed before a specific future time. For example, "By next year, he will have graduated" suggests that graduation will be completed before a future point.

- Future Perfect Continuous: Describes actions that will have been ongoing for a period up to a specific future time. For instance, "By the end of this month, they will have been working on the project for a year" indicates a continuous action reaching a future point.

3.3.3 Verb Usage and Agreement

Correct usage and agreement of verbs are essential for grammatical accuracy and clarity. Verbs must agree with their subjects in number (singular or plural) and person (first, second, third). For instance, in "She runs every morning," the singular subject "She" agrees with the singular verb "runs." In "They run every morning," the plural subject "They" agrees with the plural verb "run." Ensuring correct verb agreement helps maintain consistency and coherence in sentences.

1. Common Errors with Verbs

Several common errors can occur with verbs, including issues with tense consistency, subject-verb agreement, and incorrect verb forms.

- Tense Consistency Errors: Mixing different tenses within a sentence or paragraph can create confusion.

For example, "She was going to the store and buys groceries" incorrectly mixes past and present tenses. Maintaining consistent tense usage is crucial for clear and coherent writing.

- Subject-Verb Agreement Errors: Errors in matching verbs with their subjects can disrupt sentence agreement. For instance, saying "The group are arriving" instead of "The group is arriving" can affect grammatical correctness. Ensuring that verbs correctly agree with their subjects is essential for accurate communication.

- Incorrect Verb Forms: Using incorrect verb forms, such as mixing past and present participles or using irregular verbs incorrectly, can lead to errors. For example, "She has went to the store" should be "She has gone to the store." Correct use of verb forms is crucial for proper grammar.

2. Practical Exercises and Activities

To reinforce understanding of verbs and their tenses, students can engage in various practical exercises and activities. These might include identifying and correcting verb tense errors, creating sentences using different verb forms, and practicing verb conjugation. For example, students could be given sentences with missing verbs and asked to fill in the blanks with the correct tense. Group activities, such as verb tense quizzes or role-playing scenarios, can also enhance learning and provide opportunities for practical application.

3. Visual Aids and Resources

Visual aids, such as verb charts and tense timelines, can be helpful in teaching verbs and their tenses. A chart illustrating different verb forms and their tenses can aid in understanding and memorizing conjugations. Additionally, interactive grammar tools and online exercises can offer additional practice and support, helping students apply their knowledge in various contexts and reinforcing their understanding of verbs.

Conclusion

In summary, Chapter 3.3 of "The Fundamentals of English Grammar for Grades 5-10" provides an in-depth exploration of verbs, focusing on their types and tenses. By understanding action verbs, linking verbs, and auxiliary verbs, students can effectively construct sentences that convey clear and precise meanings. Mastery of verb tenses—present, past, and future, along with their simple, continuous, perfect, and perfect continuous forms—is essential for expressing actions and states accurately. Practical exercises and visual aids further support learning and application, enhancing students' proficiency in using verbs to create coherent and grammatically correct sentences. Through this comprehensive examination of verbs, students gain the skills necessary for effective communication and writing in English.

3.4 Adjectives: Types and Usage

In "The Fundamentals of English Grammar for Grades 5-10," the focus is on adjectives, which are integral to enhancing the clarity and detail of written and spoken language. Adjectives are words that describe or modify nouns and pronouns, providing additional information about them, such as their quality, quantity, or state. This chapter delves into the various types of adjectives and their usage, offering a thorough understanding of how adjectives function to enrich communication.

3.4.1 Types of Adjectives

Adjectives can be categorized into several types based on the specific functions they perform. These include descriptive adjectives, quantitative adjectives, demonstrative adjectives, possessive adjectives, interrogative adjectives, and comparative and superlative adjectives. Each type plays a unique role in modifying nouns and pronouns, contributing to the overall meaning of sentences.

- **Descriptive Adjectives**

Descriptive adjectives provide details about a noun or pronoun, such as color, size, shape, or other qualities. For example, in the phrase "a tall building," the adjective "tall" describes the height of the building. Descriptive adjectives are essential for painting a vivid picture and offering precise information. They help to specify attributes and characteristics, making the description more engaging and informative. For instance, "The old, wooden chair" uses the adjectives "old" and "wooden" to give more detail about the chair's appearance and material.

- **Quantitative Adjectives**

Quantitative adjectives indicate the amount or quantity of a noun. They answer questions such as "How many?" or "How much?" Examples of quantitative adjectives include "several," "few," "many," "much," "all," and "some."

For instance, in "She has three cats," the adjective "three" specifies the number of cats. Quantitative adjectives are crucial for providing information about the extent or quantity of something, helping to clarify and quantify the nouns they modify.

- **Demonstrative Adjectives**

Demonstrative adjectives point to specific nouns and indicate their relative position in space or time. They include "this," "that," "these," and "those." For example, in "I want that book," the adjective "that" specifies a particular book being referred to. Demonstrative adjectives help in identifying and distinguishing particular items or people from others, thereby adding clarity and specificity to communication.

- **Possessive Adjectives**

Possessive adjectives indicate ownership or relationship and modify nouns by showing who something belongs to. They include "my," "your," "his," "her," "its," "our," and "their." For example, in "His car is parked outside," the adjective "his" shows that the car belongs to him. Possessive adjectives are essential for expressing relationships and ownership, providing context about the connections between people and things.

- **Interrogative Adjectives**

Interrogative adjectives are used to ask questions about nouns and are typically used in interrogative sentences. They include "which," "what," and "whose." For example, in "Which dress are you wearing?" the adjective "which" is used to inquire about a specific dress. Interrogative adjectives help in seeking specific information about nouns, guiding the listener or reader to provide particular details.

- **Comparative and Superlative Adjectives**

Comparative and superlative adjectives are used to compare nouns and show differences in degrees of a particular quality. Comparative adjectives compare two nouns and are typically formed by adding "-er" to the adjective or using "more" before it. For example, "taller" is the comparative form of "tall," as in "She is taller than her sister." Superlative adjectives indicate the highest degree of a quality among three or more nouns and are formed by adding "-est" or using "most" before the adjective. For instance, "tallest" is the superlative form of "tall," as in "He is the tallest in the class."

3.4.2 Usage of Adjectives

The effective use of adjectives involves placing them correctly within sentences to ensure clarity and coherence. Adjectives typically appear before the noun they modify, as in "a beautiful sunset." However, adjectives can also follow linking verbs to describe the subject, as in "The sunset is beautiful." When multiple adjectives are used, they usually follow a specific order: quantity, quality, size, age, shape, color, origin, material, and purpose. For example, in "She wore a lovely little red dress," the adjectives "lovely," "little," and "red" follow the conventional order to provide a clear and detailed description.

1. Common Errors with Adjectives

Several common errors can occur with adjectives, including issues with adjective order, overuse, and incorrect comparative and superlative forms. Adjective order errors occur when adjectives are placed in an incorrect sequence, leading to confusion. For example, "a blue old car" should be "an old blue car." Overuse of adjectives can result in wordiness and reduce the effectiveness of descriptions. For instance, using too many adjectives, such as "a very big, huge, enormous house," can be redundant. Incorrect comparative and superlative forms, such as "more better" instead of "better," can lead to grammatical inaccuracies. Ensuring proper adjective placement, avoiding excessive use, and using correct forms are essential for clear and effective writing.

2. Practical Exercises and Activities

To reinforce understanding of adjectives and their usage, students can engage in various practical exercises and activities. These might include identifying and correcting adjective errors, creating sentences using different types of adjectives, and practicing adjective order. For example, students could be given sentences with missing adjectives and asked to fill in the blanks with appropriate descriptive words. Group discussions and peer reviews can also provide opportunities for collaborative learning and feedback on adjective usage.

3. Visual Aids and Resources

Visual aids, such as adjective charts and descriptive writing prompts, can be helpful in teaching adjectives. A chart illustrating different types of adjectives and their functions can aid in understanding and memorizing their roles. Additionally, interactive grammar tools and online exercises can offer additional practice and support, helping students apply their knowledge in various contexts and reinforcing their understanding of adjectives.

Conclusion

In "The Fundamentals of English Grammar for Grades 5-10" provides a comprehensive exploration of adjectives, focusing on their types and usage. By understanding descriptive, quantitative, demonstrative, possessive, interrogative, and comparative and superlative adjectives, students can effectively modify nouns and pronouns to add detail and clarity to their communication. Mastery of adjective placement, order, and usage is crucial for creating vivid and precise descriptions in writing and speaking. Practical exercises and visual aids further support learning and application, enhancing students' proficiency in using adjectives to enrich their language skills. Through this detailed examination of adjectives, students gain the tools necessary for effective and engaging communication in English.

3.5 Adverbs: Types and Usage

In "The Fundamentals of English Grammar for Grades 5-10," the focus shifts to adverbs, which play a crucial role in modifying verbs, adjectives, and other adverbs to provide additional detail and context. Adverbs are versatile words that enhance sentences by describing how, when, where, and to what extent actions occur. This section explores the various types of adverbs and their usage, shedding light on their function in enriching language.

3.5.1 Types of Adverbs

Adverbs are categorized based on the type of information they convey. The primary types include adverbs of manner, time, place, frequency, and degree. Each type serves a specific purpose in modifying different elements of a sentence.

- **Adverbs of Manner**

Adverbs of manner describe how an action is performed. They answer the question "How?" and typically modify verbs. For example, in the sentence "She sings beautifully," the adverb "beautifully" explains the manner in which she sings. Adverbs of manner often end in "-ly," such as "quickly," "carefully," and "loudly," but there are exceptions like "well" and "fast."

- **Adverbs of Time**

Adverbs of time provide information about when an action occurs. They answer the question "When?" and can describe actions occurring at specific times or intervals.

For instance, "We will leave tomorrow" uses the adverb "tomorrow" to indicate the time of departure. Other examples include "now," "yesterday," "soon," and "often," which help situate actions within a temporal framework.

- **Adverbs of Place**

Adverbs of place describe the location or direction of an action. They answer the question "Where?" and modify verbs to indicate where an action takes place. For example, in "The cat is sleeping outside," the adverb "outside" specifies the location of the cat's sleep. Other adverbs of place include "here," "there," "nearby," and "everywhere," which help pinpoint the spatial context of actions.

- **Adverbs of Frequency**

Adverbs of frequency indicate how often an action occurs. They answer the question "How often?" and provide insight into the regularity or occurrence of actions. For example, "She always arrives early" uses the adverb "always" to show that the action of arriving happens regularly. Other examples include "never," "seldom," "frequently," and "sometimes," which convey varying degrees of frequency.

- **Adverbs of Degree**

Adverbs of degree describe the intensity or extent of an action, adjective, or adverb. They answer the question "To what extent?" and modify verbs, adjectives, or other adverbs to provide more detail. For instance, in "He is extremely talented," the adverb "extremely" modifies the adjective "talented" to indicate a high degree of talent. Other adverbs of degree include "very," "quite," "barely," and "too," which adjust the intensity of the words they modify.

3.5.2 Usage of Adverbs

Correct usage of adverbs involves placing them appropriately within sentences to convey clear and precise meanings. Adverbs generally appear close to the word they modify, whether it is a verb, adjective, or another adverb. For example, "She dances gracefully" places the adverb "gracefully" near the verb "dances" to describe how she dances. When multiple adverbs are used, they follow a specific order: manner, place, frequency, time, and degree. For instance, "He runs quickly to the park every morning" follows this order to provide a complete description of the action.

1. Common Errors with Adverbs

Common errors with adverbs include incorrect placement, confusion with adjectives, and overuse. Misplacing adverbs can lead to ambiguity, such as in "She quickly ran to the store" versus "She ran quickly to the store." Confusing adverbs with adjectives, such as using "slow" instead of "slowly," can affect grammatical accuracy. Overusing adverbs can lead to wordiness and reduce the impact of writing, as seen in "She spoke very loudly and quite angrily," which might be simplified for clarity.

In summary, provides a thorough examination of adverbs, emphasizing their types and usage. By understanding adverbs of manner, time, place, frequency, and degree, students can enhance their ability to describe actions, qualities, and conditions with greater precision. Mastery of adverb placement and usage ensures clear and effective communication, enriching both written and spoken language.

3.6 Prepositions

In "The Fundamentals of English Grammar for Grades 5-10," prepositions are explored as essential components of sentence structure that indicate relationships between different elements within a sentence. Prepositions are words that link nouns, pronouns, or phrases to other words in a sentence, helping to clarify the spatial, temporal, and logical relationships between them. They answer questions such as "Where?" "When?" and "How?" by providing context about the position or direction of actions and objects.

3.6.1 Types and Functions of Prepositions

Prepositions can be categorized into several types based on the relationships they express. Common types include prepositions of place, time, direction, and manner. Prepositions of place, such as "in," "on," and "under," describe the location of an object relative to another, as in "The cat is on the table." Prepositions of time, such as "at," "during," and "before," specify when something happens, as in "We will meet at noon." Prepositions of direction, such as "to," "toward," and "through," indicate movement or direction, as in "She walked to the park." Prepositions of manner, like "by," "with," and "like," describe how an action is performed, as in "He wrote with a pen."

3.6.2 Usage of Prepositions

The correct usage of prepositions is crucial for constructing clear and grammatically accurate sentences. Prepositions typically precede nouns or pronouns, forming prepositional phrases that add detail and context. For example, in the sentence "The book is on the shelf," the prepositional phrase "on the shelf" provides information about the location of the book. It is important to choose the appropriate preposition to convey the intended meaning accurately, as different prepositions can change the context or clarity of a sentence. For instance, "She is interested in art" versus "She is interested on art" demonstrates how using the wrong preposition can lead to grammatical errors.

3.6.3 Common Errors with Prepositions

Common errors with prepositions include using incorrect prepositions, omitting necessary prepositions, and misplacing prepositions. For instance, saying "She arrived to the station" instead of "She arrived at the station" is an error in prepositional choice. Omitting prepositions can lead to incomplete or unclear sentences, such as "He is responsible the project" instead of "He is responsible for the project." Misplacing prepositions, such as in "The dog sat the chair on," can disrupt sentence structure and clarity. Ensuring correct prepositional use enhances readability and precision in writing and speaking.

Conclusion

In summary, prepositions are fundamental to establishing clear and coherent relationships within sentences. They provide critical context about location, time, direction, and manner, enriching the meaning of sentences. Mastery of prepositions involves understanding their types, functions, and proper usage to create grammatically correct and effective communication. Through careful selection and placement of prepositions, students can improve their language skills and convey their intended messages with greater accuracy and clarity.

3.7 Conjunctions

Conjunctions are pivotal in linking words, phrases, and clauses to form coherent and unified sentences. They serve as connectors that establish logical relationships and smooth transitions between various elements within a sentence. By coordinating, subordinating, or correlating different parts of speech, conjunctions help create complete and meaningful expressions.

- **Coordinating Conjunctions**

Coordinating conjunctions are used to connect words, phrases, or clauses of equal importance. They are essential for constructing compound sentences and ensuring balance within the sentence structure. The most common coordinating conjunctions are "for," "and," "nor," "but," "or," "yet," and "so." For instance, in the sentence "She wanted to go to the park, but it started to rain," the conjunction "but" links two independent clauses, showing a contrast between the desire to visit the park and the reality of the rain. Coordinating conjunctions are fundamental for creating compound sentences that present related ideas and maintain grammatical symmetry.

- **Subordinating Conjunctions**

Subordinating conjunctions connect dependent clauses to independent clauses, establishing a relationship where one clause relies on the other for complete meaning. These conjunctions provide additional context and detail, enhancing the information conveyed by the main clause. Common subordinating conjunctions include "because," "although," "since," "while," and "if." For example, in the sentence "She stayed home because it was raining," the conjunction "because" introduces a reason for the action described in the main clause. Subordinating conjunctions are crucial for forming complex sentences that provide more nuanced and detailed information.

- **Correlative Conjunctions**

Correlative conjunctions work in pairs to connect equal elements within a sentence, ensuring balance and parallelism. Examples of correlative pairs include "either...or," "neither...nor," "both...and," "not only...but also," and "whether...or." For example, in "Both the manager and the assistant attended the meeting," the pair "both...and" links two subjects, emphasizing their joint participation. Correlative conjunctions are vital for maintaining grammatical symmetry and clarity, helping to create sentences that are balanced and coherent.

3.7.1 Usage and Importance of Conjunctions

The effective use of conjunctions is essential for constructing clear and coherent sentences. Coordinating conjunctions enable the formation of compound sentences that link related ideas, while subordinating conjunctions add depth by combining dependent and independent clauses. Correlative conjunctions ensure that linked elements are balanced and parallel, enhancing readability and flow.

Proper conjunction usage helps avoid sentence fragments and run-on sentences, contributing to more polished and effective communication. By providing clear connections between ideas, conjunctions prevent ambiguity and improve the overall clarity of writing.

1. Common Errors with Conjunctions

Errors with conjunctions can undermine sentence clarity and grammatical correctness. Common mistakes include incorrect pairing of correlative conjunctions, overuse of coordinating conjunctions, and improper separation of clauses. For instance, using "both...and" with only one element, as in "Both the teacher and attended the conference," results in an incomplete structure. Overusing coordinating conjunctions, such as excessive "ands," can lead to lengthy and cumbersome sentences. Additionally, failing to separate clauses correctly can result in run-on sentences, such as "She wanted to go for a walk she was too tired."

In summary, conjunctions are essential tools for linking various elements within sentences, facilitating clear and coherent communication. By mastering the use of coordinating, subordinating, and correlative conjunctions, individuals can enhance their ability to construct well-structured sentences that accurately convey their intended meanings. Effective use of conjunctions contributes to grammatical correctness and improved writing skills, making it a fundamental aspect of proficient language use.

3.8 Interjections

Interjections are distinctive elements of language used to express strong emotions, reactions, or exclamations. They serve as spontaneous outbursts or interruptions in the flow of a sentence, providing a way to convey immediate feelings or responses without grammatical connections to other parts of the sentence. Unlike other parts of speech, interjections stand alone or are inserted into sentences to emphasize emotions or reactions, rather than to perform grammatical functions.

3.8.1 Definition and Function

An interjection is a word or phrase that conveys an emotional reaction or exclamation. It is typically used to express feelings such as surprise, joy, pain, excitement, or other intense emotions. Interjections often stand apart from the main sentence structure and are usually followed by an exclamation mark or, in some cases, a comma.

For instance, "Wow! That was an amazing performance!" uses the interjection "Wow" to express astonishment and enthusiasm about the performance.

3.8.2 Types of Interjections

Interjections can be categorized based on the type of emotion or reaction they express:

1. **Exclamatory Interjections**: These are used to express strong feelings or reactions and are commonly followed by an exclamation mark. Examples include "Oh," "Wow," "Ouch," and "Yikes." For example, "Ouch! That really hurt" uses "Ouch" to convey pain and surprise.

2. **Greeting Interjections**: These are used to greet someone or to address a person. Common examples include "Hello," "Hi," "Hey," and "Goodbye." For instance, "Hello! How have you been?" uses "Hello" as a greeting.

3. **Response Interjections**: These indicate a response to something said or an acknowledgment. Examples include "Yes," "No," "Uh-huh," and "Hmm." For example, "Yes, I understand what

you mean" uses "Yes" to affirm understanding.

4. Attention Interjections: These are used to draw attention or prompt someone to listen. Examples include "Listen," "Hey," and "Look." For instance, "Hey, look at this!" uses "Hey" to capture attention.

3.8.3 Usage of Interjections

Interjections are usually placed at the beginning of a sentence or phrase, but they can also be found in the middle or at the end, depending on their function and the emotional emphasis required. They are often set off by punctuation marks such as commas or exclamation points to convey the nature and intensity of the emotion. For example, "Oh, I forgot to bring my book" uses "Oh" to express a sudden realization or mild surprise. Effective use of interjections can enhance communication by adding emotional nuance and engaging the listener or reader more deeply.

- **Common Errors with Interjections**

Common mistakes with interjections include improper punctuation, overuse, and incorrect placement. For instance, failing to use appropriate punctuation, such as writing "Wow that was amazing" instead of "Wow! That was amazing," can weaken the impact of the interjection. Overusing interjections, such as in "Wow, wow, wow! That was so amazing!" can make communication seem overly dramatic or cluttered.

Misplacing interjections within sentences, such as in "That was, wow, an incredible performance," can disrupt the flow and clarity of the message. Ensuring correct punctuation and appropriate usage helps maintain the effectiveness of interjections in communication.

Conclusion

Interjections are crucial for expressing immediate emotions and reactions in a vivid and engaging manner. They add emotional depth and spontaneity to both spoken and written language, helping to convey the speaker's or writer's feelings effectively. By understanding the different types of interjections and their proper usage, individuals can enhance their ability to communicate with greater expressiveness and clarity, enriching their overall language skills.

CHAPTER - 4

SENTENCE STRUCTURE

4. Introduction of Sentence Structure

Sentence structure is a fundamental aspect of writing that influences clarity, readability, and overall effectiveness of communication. It refers to the way in which words, phrases, and clauses are arranged to form sentences. Proper sentence structure ensures that ideas are conveyed clearly and logically, allowing the reader to follow and understand the writer's message with ease. At the core of sentence structure is the basic sentence pattern, which typically includes a subject and a predicate. The subject of a sentence is the noun, pronoun, or noun phrase that the sentence is about. It is the actor or the topic being discussed. The predicate contains the verb and provides information about what the subject is doing or what is happening to the subject.

For instance, in the sentence "The dog barked loudly," "The dog" is the subject, and "barked loudly" is the predicate. This simple structure forms the foundation of more complex sentences. Sentence types can be classified based on their structure and function. Simple sentences contain a single independent clause, which expresses a complete thought. They are straightforward and contain a subject and a predicate. For example, "She reads books" is a simple sentence with a clear subject ("She") and predicate ("reads books"). Despite their simplicity, simple sentences are crucial for clarity and directness. Compound sentences consist of two or more independent clauses joined by coordinating conjunctions such as "and," "but," "or," "nor," "for," "so," or "yet." Each independent clause in a compound sentence can stand alone as a complete sentence.

For instance, "I wanted to go for a walk, but it started raining" combines two independent clauses, "I wanted to go for a walk" and "it started raining," using the conjunction "but" to link them. Compound sentences allow for more complex expressions by connecting related ideas. Complex sentences feature one independent clause and at least one dependent clause. A dependent clause provides additional information but cannot stand alone as a complete sentence. For example, in the sentence "Although it was raining, we decided to go for a walk," "Although it was raining" is the dependent clause, and "we decided to go for a walk" is the independent clause. Complex sentences enable writers to convey nuanced relationships between ideas, showing cause and effect, contrast, or condition. Compound-complex sentences combine elements of both compound and complex sentences.

They contain at least two independent clauses and one or more dependent clauses. An example is "I wanted to go for a walk, but because it was raining, we stayed indoors." This sentence includes two independent clauses ("I wanted to go for a walk" and "we stayed indoors") and a dependent clause ("because it was raining"), providing a richer, more detailed expression of ideas. Sentence length and complexity can vary greatly. Short sentences are effective for conveying clear and direct information or creating emphasis. They are often used to highlight important points or to break up more complex sentences for readability. Longer sentences, on the other hand, can provide detailed descriptions or elaborate on intricate ideas.

However, excessively long sentences may become convoluted and difficult to follow. Striking a balance between short and long sentences helps maintain reader engagement and ensures clarity. Sentence fragments are incomplete sentences that lack a subject, predicate, or both. They often occur when a dependent clause is mistakenly written as a standalone sentence. For example, "Although he was late" is a fragment that needs completion, such as "Although he was late, he still made it to the meeting." Fragments can disrupt the flow of writing and should be corrected to form complete, coherent sentences. Run-on sentences occur when two or more independent clauses are improperly joined without appropriate punctuation or conjunctions. For instance, "I went to the store I bought milk" is a run-on sentence that should be corrected to "I went to the store, and I bought milk."

Proper use of commas, semicolons, or conjunctions helps avoid run-on sentences and ensures grammatical correctness Modifiers are words or phrases that provide additional detail about other elements in a sentence. Misplaced or dangling modifiers can lead to ambiguity or confusion. For example, "Running to catch the bus, the rain soaked my clothes" incorrectly suggests that the rain is running. The correct structure should be "Running to catch the bus, I got soaked by the rain." Proper placement of modifiers ensures that sentences are clear and that descriptive information accurately reflects the intended meaning.

Parallel structure involves using the same grammatical pattern within a sentence to enhance readability and cohesion. For example, in the sentence "She enjoys reading, writing, and swimming," the use of the same gerund form ("reading," "writing," "swimming") creates a balanced and harmonious structure. Consistent use of parallelism helps in emphasizing points and improves the overall flow of writing. Sentence variety is important for maintaining reader interest and avoiding monotony. Utilizing a mix of sentence types, lengths, and structures can create a more engaging and dynamic writing style.

For instance, alternating between simple, compound, and complex sentences can provide rhythm and enhance the readability of the text. In summary, sentence structure encompasses the arrangement of words, phrases, and clauses to form coherent and effective communication. Understanding the basic components, including subject and predicate, and the various types of sentences—simple, compound, complex, and compound-complex—helps in crafting clear and engaging writing. Balancing sentence length, avoiding fragments and run-ons, placing modifiers correctly, and maintaining parallel structure are key to producing polished and professional text. Effective sentence structure not only conveys ideas clearly but also enhances the reader's experience and understanding.

5.1 Simple Sentences

A simple sentence is a fundamental aspect of sentence structure, providing the basic building blocks for more complex forms of communication. In the context of English grammar, understanding simple sentences is essential for developing a solid foundation in language usage and comprehension. A simple sentence consists of a single independent clause, containing a subject and a predicate, and expresses a complete thought. This chapter delves into the characteristics, components, and significance of simple sentences, illustrating how they form the basis for effective communication.

- **Definition and Characteristics of Simple Sentences**

A simple sentence is defined as a sentence that contains only one independent clause. An independent clause is a group of words that includes a subject and a predicate and can stand alone as a complete sentence. Simple sentences are straightforward and convey clear, concise ideas. For example, "The cat sleeps" is a simple sentence where "The cat" is the subject and "sleeps" is the predicate.

1. Components of Simple Sentences

The primary components of a simple sentence are the subject and the predicate. The subject is the part of the sentence that tells us who or what the sentence is about. It can be a noun, pronoun, or a noun phrase. The predicate is the part of the sentence that tells us what the subject does or is. It includes the verb and any accompanying information such as objects, complements, or modifiers. For instance, in the sentence "The dog barked loudly," "The dog" is the subject, and "barked loudly" is the predicate.

2. Subject

The subject of a simple sentence can be a single noun or pronoun, as in "Birds fly," or it can be a compound subject, where two or more subjects share the same predicate, as in "John and Mary went to the market." Compound subjects add variety to simple sentences while maintaining their straightforward structure.

3. Predicate

The predicate can also vary in complexity. It can be a simple verb, such as in "He runs," or it can include objects and complements, as in "She reads a book." Additionally, the predicate can include modifiers that provide more information about the action or state of the subject. For example, "The child plays joyfully in the garden" includes the verb "plays," the adverb "joyfully," and the prepositional phrase "in the garden."

4. Significance of Simple Sentences

- **Clarity**: Simple sentences are clear and direct, making them easy to understand. They are particularly useful for conveying straightforward information without ambiguity.

- **Foundation for Complexity**: Understanding simple sentences is fundamental for learning more complex sentence structures. They serve as the building blocks for compound, complex, and compound-complex sentences.

- **Emphasis**: Simple sentences can be used to emphasize a point or highlight a specific piece of information. Their brevity can draw attention to the core message, making it more impactful.

- **Variety in Writing:** While simple sentences alone might be too basic for advanced writing, they add variety when combined with more complex sentences. This variation can enhance the readability and flow of a text.

5. Examples of Simple Sentences

- "The sun rises."
- "She dances beautifully."
- "Children play in the park."
- "The teacher explains the lesson."
- "Birds sing in the morning."

Conclusion

Simple sentences are the foundation of English grammar, providing clarity and directness in communication. By mastering the construction and use of simple sentences, learners can build a strong grammatical foundation that will support their development of more complex sentence structures. Understanding and utilizing simple sentences effectively is essential for clear and effective communication, both in writing and speaking. Through practice and application, students can enhance their language skills and express their ideas with confidence and precision.

5.2 Compound Sentences

A compound sentence is a crucial element of sentence structure that combines two or more independent clauses to form a single, cohesive sentence. Unlike simple sentences, which contain only one independent clause, compound sentences link multiple clauses, each of which could stand alone as a complete sentence. Understanding compound sentences is essential for creating more varied and sophisticated written and spoken communication. This section explores the definition, structure, usage, and significance of compound sentences, providing examples and insights into their correct construction.

- **Definition and Characteristics of Compound Sentences**

A compound sentence is formed by joining two or more independent clauses. An independent clause is a group of words that contains a subject and a predicate and expresses a complete thought. Each independent clause in a compound sentence can stand alone as a separate simple sentence, but when combined, they provide a more complex and nuanced expression of ideas. For example, "I wanted to go for a walk, but it started to rain" is a compound sentence where each clause could be a simple sentence on its own: "I wanted to go for a walk." and "It started to rain."

1. **Components of Compound Sentences**

The primary components of a compound sentence are the

independent clauses and the conjunctions or punctuation that join them. There are several ways to link independent clauses in a compound sentence:

- **Coordinating Conjunctions**: The most common method of joining independent clauses is through coordinating conjunctions. These conjunctions include "for," "and," "nor," "but," "or," "yet," and "so" (often remembered by the acronym FANBOYS). A comma is typically placed before the coordinating conjunction. For example, "She enjoys reading, and she loves writing."

- **Semicolons**: Independent clauses can also be joined by a semicolon when the ideas are closely related and the clauses are balanced. For example, "I wanted to play outside; the weather was perfect." A semicolon provides a stronger pause than a comma but indicates a closer connection between the clauses than a period.

- **Conjunctive Adverbs**: Another method of joining independent clauses is through the use of conjunctive adverbs such as "however," "therefore," "moreover," and "consequently." A semicolon is placed before the conjunctive adverb, and a comma follows it. For example, "She studied hard for the exam; however, she still found it challenging."

2. Compound sentences are vital for several reasons:

- **Variety and Complexity**: Using compound sentences adds variety to writing and speech, preventing monotonous repetition of simple sentences. They allow for the combination of related ideas, making communication more engaging and sophisticated.

- **Logical Relationships**: Compound sentences help to show the relationship between different ideas or actions. Coordinating conjunctions and conjunctive adverbs indicate whether the clauses are adding information, contrasting, showing cause and effect, or providing alternatives.

- **Clarity and Emphasis**: By linking related independent clauses, compound sentences can emphasize connections between ideas and provide clearer, more detailed explanations. For example, "He was tired, so he went to bed early" clearly explains the cause and effect relationship between being tired and going to bed early.

Conclusion

Compound sentences are essential tools for effective communication, enabling the combination of related ideas into more complex and nuanced expressions. By mastering the use of coordinating conjunctions, semicolons, and conjunctive adverbs, learners can enhance their writing and speaking skills, creating more engaging, varied, and sophisticated sentences.

Understanding and using compound sentences correctly is crucial for achieving clarity, coherence, and variety in language, making it an indispensable aspect of advanced grammar proficiency.

5.3 Complex Sentences

A complex sentence is a critical component of sentence structure that enhances the depth and intricacy of written and spoken communication. Unlike simple and compound sentences, which contain only independent clauses, a complex sentence includes at least one independent clause and one or more dependent clauses. Understanding and using complex sentences effectively is essential for conveying detailed and nuanced ideas, making communication more engaging and sophisticated. This section explores the definition, structure, usage, and significance of complex sentences, providing examples and insights into their correct construction.

- **Definition and Characteristics of Complex Sentences**

A complex sentence is defined as a sentence that includes one independent clause and at least one dependent clause. An independent clause is a group of words that contains a subject and a predicate and can stand alone as a complete sentence. A dependent clause, also known as a subordinate clause, also contains a subject and a predicate but cannot stand alone as a complete sentence. Dependent clauses rely on the main independent clause to provide context and meaning. For example, "Although it was raining, we decided to go for a walk" is a complex sentence where "Although it was raining" is the dependent clause and "we decided to go for a walk" is the independent clause.

1. **Components of Complex Sentences**

The primary components of a complex sentence are the independent clause and the dependent clause(s). These clauses are connected in a way that indicates the relationship between the ideas they express. There are several types of dependent clauses, each serving a specific function:

- **Adverbial Clauses**: These clauses act as adverbs, providing information about when, where, why, how, or under what conditions the action of the main clause occurs. They are introduced by subordinating conjunctions such as "although," "because," "if," "since," "unless," "when," "while," and "after." For example, "Because she was tired, she went to bed early" uses the adverbial clause "Because she was tired" to explain the reason for the action in the main clause.

- **Relative Clauses**: Also known as adjective clauses, these clauses provide more information about a noun or pronoun in the main clause. They are introduced by relative pronouns such as "who," "whom," "whose," "which," and "that." For instance, "The book that I borrowed from the library is fascinating" includes the relative clause "that I borrowed from the library," which describes the noun "book."

- **Noun Clauses**: These clauses function as nouns within the sentence and can act as subjects, objects, or complements. They are introduced by words like "that," "what," "whatever," "who," "whom," and "whether." For example, "What he said was surprising" uses the noun clause "What he said" as the subject of the sentence.

2. **Usage and Significance of Complex Sentences**

- **Depth and Detail**: Complex sentences allow writers and speakers to provide more detailed and nuanced information. They can explain reasons, conditions, time, and relationships between ideas, making communication richer and more informative.

- **Clarity and Precision**: By combining related ideas into a single sentence, complex sentences help to clarify relationships and ensure that the intended meaning is conveyed precisely. This is particularly useful in academic and professional writing, where clarity and detail are essential.

- **Engagement and Variety**: Using complex sentences adds variety to writing and speech, preventing monotonous repetition of simple and compound sentences. They create a more engaging and dynamic flow of ideas, capturing the reader's or listener's attention.

Each of these sentences includes at least one independent clause and one dependent clause, demonstrating how complex sentences can convey detailed and related ideas effectively. Despite their advantages, complex sentences can be challenging to construct correctly. Common errors include:

1. **Fragmented Sentences**: A dependent clause standing alone is a fragment and not a complete sentence. For example, "Because she was late." should be corrected to "Because she was late, she missed the bus."

2. **Comma Misuse**: Incorrectly placing or omitting commas can lead to confusion. For example, "She went to the store because she needed milk, and eggs" should be "She went to the store because she needed milk and eggs" or "She went to the store because she needed milk, and she bought eggs."

3. **Misplaced Clauses**: Placing a dependent clause in the wrong part of the sentence can alter the intended meaning. For example, "He said on Monday he would come" should be "He said he would come on Monday" to clarify the time.

Conclusion

Complex sentences are essential tools for conveying detailed, nuanced, and related ideas in a single, coherent sentence. By mastering the use of adverbial, relative, and noun clauses, learners can enhance their writing and speaking skills, creating more engaging, precise, and varied sentences. Understanding and using complex sentences correctly is crucial for achieving clarity, depth, and sophistication in communication, making it an indispensable aspect of advanced grammar proficiency.

CHAPTER - 5

PUNCTUATION AND CAPITALIZATION

6Introduction of Punctuation and Capitalization

Punctuation and capitalization are essential elements of written language that help clarify meaning, indicate pauses, and convey the correct tone and structure of sentences. Mastery of these elements ensures that text is readable, coherent, and professional, facilitating effective communication. Punctuation marks are symbols used to organize written language and provide readers with cues on how to interpret sentences. They help delineate ideas, indicate pauses, and separate different elements within a sentence. The most common punctuation marks include periods, commas, question marks, exclamation marks, colons, semicolons, quotation marks, and apostrophes. Periods are used to indicate the end of a declarative sentence, signaling a full stop.

They are fundamental for completing statements, such as in "She enjoys reading." Periods also follow abbreviations, like "Dr." or "Inc." The consistent use of periods helps maintain clarity by marking the end of a complete thought.Commas are versatile punctuation marks used to separate elements within a sentence, such as items in a list, clauses, or adjectives. For example, in "I bought apples, oranges, and bananas," commas separate the items in the list. Commas are also used after introductory elements, like "After the meeting, we went for lunch," and to set off non-essential information, such as "My brother, who lives in New York, is visiting us." Question marks are employed at the end of direct questions, such as "What time is the meeting?"

They indicate an interrogative sentence and prompt the reader to consider the query being posed. Using question marks appropriately helps in distinguishing between questions and statements, enhancing the clarity of the text. Exclamation marks convey strong emotions or emphasis and are placed at the end of sentences that express excitement, surprise, or urgency, such as "Wow, that's amazing!" While exclamation marks add intensity to the writing, overusing them can diminish their effectiveness and make the text appear overly dramatic. Colons are used to introduce lists, explanations, or quotations. They precede items in a list or a detailed explanation, as in "She brought three items: a notebook, a pen, and a water bottle." Colons are also used before a quotation that follows a complete sentence, such as "He said it best:

'The journey of a thousand miles begins with a single step.'" Semicolons connect closely related independent clauses that are not joined by a conjunction. For example, "She loves chocolate; he prefers vanilla." Semicolons can also be used to separate items in a complex list where commas alone might create confusion, such as "The conference attendees included Jane Smith, the CEO; John Doe, the CFO; and Emily Johnson, the COO." Quotation marks enclose direct speech, quotations, or titles of short works. For instance, "The professor said, 'Please submit your assignments by Friday.'" They are also used to indicate irony or unusual usage, as in "He claimed to be 'the expert' on the subject." Apostrophes indicate possession or form contractions. For possession, they show ownership, as in "Sarah's book" (the book belonging to Sarah) or "the children's toys" (the toys belonging to the children).

Apostrophes are also used in contractions to replace omitted letters, such as "don't" (do not) or "it's" (it is). Capitalization involves using uppercase letters to denote specific grammatical and stylistic elements in writing. Proper nouns, such as names of people, places, and organizations, are capitalized to distinguish them from common nouns. For example, "New York City" and "Microsoft" are capitalized because they refer to specific entities. The first word of a sentence is always capitalized, marking the beginning of a new thought or statement. This practice ensures that readers can easily identify the start of a sentence, enhancing readability. For instance, "The dog ran quickly across the field." Titles of works, such as books, movies, and articles, are capitalized according to specific formatting rules. In titles, the first and last words are always capitalized, along with important words in between, such as "To Kill a Mockingbird" or "The Great Gatsby." Days of the week, months of the year, and holidays are capitalized to signify specific time periods, as in "Monday," "January," and "Christmas." These capitalizations help in distinguishing these time-related terms from general references. Personal titles used before names, such as "Mr.," "Dr.," or "President," are capitalized to denote respect and formality, as in "Dr. Smith" or "President Lincoln." However, when titles are used generically or after names, they are not capitalized, as in "the president of the company." Pronouns referring to God are capitalized to convey reverence, such as "He" or "Him" when referring to the deity in religious contexts. This practice shows respect and acknowledges the divine nature of the subject. Proper use of punctuation and capitalization is vital for clear and effective writing. Punctuation marks guide readers through the text, indicating pauses, separating ideas, and clarifying meaning.

Capitalization rules provide structure and signify the importance of specific words and names. Mastery of these elements ensures that writing is polished, professional, and easily understood, enhancing the overall communication experience.

5.1 Periods, Commas, Question Marks, Exclamation Points

Punctuation marks such as periods, commas, question marks, and exclamation marks are fundamental elements of written English that significantly enhance clarity, structure, and expressiveness. Each of these punctuation marks has a specific function that aids in the communication of ideas by providing necessary pauses, indicating the end of statements, and conveying emotion or inquiry. Understanding and mastering their usage is essential for effective writing. Periods are the most basic punctuation marks, used to signal the end of a declarative sentence or a mild imperative. They clearly define the boundaries of a complete thought, ensuring that each sentence is easily understood. For instance, "She walked to the store." uses a period to mark the end of the action. Periods also appear in abbreviations, such as "Dr." for "Doctor" or "Mr." for "Mister," providing clarity and precision in writing. Commas are versatile punctuation marks serving multiple purposes within a sentence. They separate items in a list, such as "We bought apples, oranges, and bananas," ensuring that each item is distinct.

Commas set off introductory elements from the main clause, as in "After the movie, we went to dinner." They also separate independent clauses joined by coordinating conjunctions like "and," "but," or "or," for example, "She wanted to go for a walk, but it started to rain." Additionally, commas enclose non-essential information or clauses, adding extra details without disrupting the flow of the sentence, such as "My brother, who lives in New York, is visiting us." Question marks indicate that a sentence is a direct question, prompting the reader to consider an inquiry or request information. They are placed at the end of interrogative sentences, transforming statements into questions. For instance, "What time is the meeting?" clearly signals a request for specific information. Question marks are essential for maintaining the interactive aspect of written communication, ensuring that questions are properly identified and answered. Exclamation marks express strong emotions or emphasis, adding intensity to a sentence. They are often found in exclamatory sentences, commands, or interjections, such as "Wow! That was amazing!" or "Stop!" Exclamation marks convey excitement, urgency, or surprise, making the writer's intended emotional tone clear to the reader.

While they can add dramatic flair to writing, it is important to use exclamation marks sparingly to avoid diminishing their impact. Proper punctuation is crucial for effective communication, as it ensures that written language is clear, accurate, and engaging. Periods provide closure and structure to sentences, commas add necessary pauses and clarify relationships between ideas, question marks denote inquiries, and exclamation marks convey strong emotions. Mastering the use of these punctuation marks allows writers to express their thoughts clearly and accurately, enhancing both the readability and impact of their writing. By understanding the roles and correct usage of periods, commas, question marks, and exclamation marks, writers can significantly improve the quality of their written communication. These punctuation marks are not merely technical elements; they are essential tools for shaping the meaning and tone of sentences, making them indispensable for anyone aiming to write effectively. Whether writing a simple message, a detailed report, or an expressive narrative, the proper use of punctuation marks ensures that the intended message is conveyed with clarity and precision.

5.2 Quotation Marks, Apostrophes, Colons, Semicolons

Quotation marks, apostrophes, colons, and semicolons are essential punctuation marks that play critical roles in enhancing the clarity, accuracy, and flow of written English. Each of these punctuation marks serves distinct purposes, contributing to the effective communication of ideas and ensuring that the intended meaning is accurately conveyed. This section explores the usage and significance of quotation marks, apostrophes, colons, and semicolons.

1. Quotation Marks

Quotation marks are used to enclose direct speech, quotations, and certain titles, distinguishing the quoted material from the rest of the text. They signal to the reader that the enclosed words are not the writer's own but are attributed to another source. For example, "She said, 'I will be there at five o'clock.'" clearly indicates that the words within the single quotes are spoken by someone else. Quotation marks are also used for titles of short works such as articles, poems, and short stories, e.g., "The Road Not Taken" by Robert Frost. In addition, they can indicate irony or skepticism, as in, She claimed she was "working" all night

2. Apostrophes

Apostrophes serve two primary functions: indicating possession and forming contractions. To show possession, an apostrophe followed by an "s" is added to the noun, as in "the dog's leash" or "James's book." For plural nouns ending in "s," only an apostrophe is added, such as "the teachers' lounge." Apostrophes are also used to form contractions, which are shortened forms of words or phrases, such as "don't" for "do not," "it's" for "it is," and "you're" for "you are." Apostrophes help to clarify meaning and ensure that sentences are concise and readable.

3. Colons

Colons are used to introduce lists, explanations, quotations, or examples, providing a pause that emphasizes the material that follows. For instance, "She brought three things to the picnic: sandwiches, fruit, and lemonade." Here, the colon introduces the list of items. Colons can also precede an explanation or elaboration, as in "He had only one goal: to win the championship." In addition, colons are used in formal letter greetings, time expressions, and bibliographic entries. For example, "Dear Dr. Smith:", "The train departs at 10:30", and "Smith, John. Understanding Grammar: A Guide for Teachers."

4. Semicolons

Semicolons are used to link closely related independent clauses and to separate items in complex lists. When linking independent clauses, semicolons suggest a closer connection between the clauses than a period would. For example, "She loves to read; her favorite author is Jane Austen." This indicates a strong relationship between the two statements. Semicolons are also used in lists where the items contain commas, to avoid confusion. For instance, "The conference included speakers from Paris, France; Tokyo, Japan; and New York,

USA." This clarifies the separation of each item in the list.

Conclusion

Mastering the use of quotation marks, apostrophes, colons, and semicolons is crucial for effective written communication. Quotation marks distinguish quoted material, apostrophes indicate possession and form contractions, colons introduce lists and explanations, and semicolons link related clauses and clarify complex lists. Each of these punctuation marks contributes to the clarity, precision, and fluidity of writing, ensuring that ideas are communicated accurately and effectively.

Understanding their proper usage allows writers to enhance their writing's readability and impact, making these punctuation marks indispensable tools in the art of writing.

5.3 Capitalization Rules

Capitalization rules are fundamental to written English, providing structure and clarity by indicating the beginning of sentences, proper nouns, titles, and specific elements within the text. Proper capitalization helps readers navigate the text more easily and understand the importance or distinctiveness of certain words. This section explores the essential rules of capitalization, offering guidance on when and how to capitalize words correctly. One of the most basic rules of capitalization is that the first word of every sentence should be capitalized. This signals the beginning of a new thought or statement, making it easier for readers to follow the flow of the text.

For example, "The cat sat on the mat." Here, the word "The" is capitalized to indicate the start of the sentence. Proper nouns, which name specific people, places, organizations, and sometimes things, should always be capitalized. This includes names of individuals like "John Smith," geographical locations like "New York City," institutions such as "Harvard University," and specific brands like "Coca-Cola." Capitalizing proper nouns distinguishes them from common nouns, which are not capitalized unless they begin a sentence or are part of a title. For instance, "The book was written by John Smith," where "John Smith" is a proper noun and is capitalized. Titles of works, including books, movies, articles, and songs, require capitalization for the main words. This typically includes the first and last words, and all major words in between, excluding short articles, conjunctions, and prepositions unless they are the first or last words of the title.

For example, "To Kill a Mockingbird" and "The Lord of the Rings" follow this rule. However, in a title like "Gone with the Wind," "with" is not capitalized because it is a short preposition not at the beginning or end of the title. When referring to specific days, months, holidays, and historical periods, capitalization is required. For example, "Monday," "July," "Christmas," and "the Renaissance" are all capitalized. This rule helps to differentiate these specific time periods from general time words, such as "day" or "month," which are not capitalized unless they begin a sentence. In addition to these basic rules, certain words should always be capitalized in specific contexts. For instance, when using titles of respect and familial relations directly before a name, they are capitalized, such as "Doctor Smith," "President Lincoln," or "Aunt Mary."

However, if these titles are used generically and not directly preceding a name, they are not capitalized: "My doctor is very kind," or "She became a president of the company." Religious terms and deities' names are also capitalized, reflecting their importance and reverence. This includes terms like "God," "Allah," "the Bible," and "the Quran." Furthermore, specific names of religions, religious movements, and followers are capitalized, such as "Christianity," "Islam," "Hinduism," "Christians," and "Muslims." Capitalization rules extend to acronyms and initialisms, which are always written in capital letters. This ensures that abbreviations of longer terms are easily recognized and properly understood. For example, "NASA" stands for the National Aeronautics and Space Administration, and "UN" stands for the United Nations. Additionally, the first letter of each major word in acronyms and initialisms that are pronounced as words (e.g., "NATO" for the North Atlantic Treaty Organization) is capitalized. In professional and academic writing, headings and subheadings are often capitalized following title case rules, similar to the capitalization of titles. This includes capitalizing the first and last words, and all major words in between, while generally not capitalizing articles, short conjunctions, and prepositions unless they are the first or last words. Understanding and correctly applying capitalization rules is essential for clear, professional, and effective writing. It ensures that proper nouns and important words are appropriately highlighted, aiding in the reader's comprehension and engagement with the text. By adhering to these rules, writers can produce well-structured and easily readable documents that communicate their ideas clearly and effectively.

CHAPTER - 6

VOCABULARY BUILDING

6 Introduction of Vocabulary Building

Vocabulary building is a crucial aspect of language development that enhances both communication skills and comprehension. It involves expanding one's repertoire of words and understanding their meanings, usages, and nuances. A rich vocabulary enables individuals to express themselves more precisely, engage more effectively in conversations, and comprehend texts more deeply. It plays a significant role in academic success, professional advancement, and personal enrichment, contributing to clearer expression and more effective communication. Building vocabulary begins with exposure to new words through various means, such as reading widely, listening actively, and engaging in discussions. Reading diverse genres—whether literature, science, or news—introduces readers to a broad array of vocabulary.

For instance, novels may introduce literary terms and descriptive language, while scientific articles might present technical jargon and specialized terminology. Each exposure helps reinforce word meanings and usage in context, aiding in retention and comprehension. Active reading techniques, such as annotating texts, using context clues, and looking up unfamiliar words, further facilitate vocabulary growth. Annotating involves making notes in the margins of a text, which can include definitions or synonyms of challenging words. Context clues, such as the surrounding text or sentence structure, provide hints about a word's meaning. When encountering unfamiliar terms, using a dictionary or thesaurus to look up definitions helps clarify their meanings and expands understanding.

Vocabulary lists and flashcards are practical tools for systematic vocabulary building. Creating lists of new words along with their definitions and example sentences allows for focused study. Flashcards, which can be physical cards or digital apps, help reinforce learning through repetition and active recall. Techniques such as spaced repetition, where words are reviewed at increasing intervals, improve long-term retention and recall. In addition to these methods, word games and puzzles can make vocabulary building enjoyable and interactive. Games like Scrabble, Boggle, and crossword puzzles challenge players to use and recognize new words, while also expanding their understanding of word forms and meanings. Engaging in such activities stimulates cognitive processes related to language and enhances vocabulary skills in a fun and engaging manner.

Learning word roots, prefixes, and suffixes is another effective strategy for vocabulary building. Understanding the components of words helps decipher unfamiliar terms and grasp their meanings. For example, knowing that the prefix "un-" means "not" and the suffix "-able" means "capable of" can help deduce the meaning of words like "unfortunate" and "manageable." This morphological knowledge builds a foundation for understanding a wide range of words and enhances the ability to infer meanings. Contextual usage of new vocabulary is crucial for mastering word meanings and incorporating them into everyday language. Practicing new words in sentences, conversations, and writing helps solidify their meanings and appropriate usage.

Engaging in discussions or writing exercises that require the use of new vocabulary not only reinforces learning but also helps integrate new terms into one's active vocabulary. Language immersion experiences, such as participating in language courses or interacting with native speakers, can accelerate vocabulary acquisition. Immersion provides practical experience with language, offering opportunities to use and encounter new words in authentic contexts. This hands-on approach enhances comprehension and retention, making vocabulary learning more dynamic and effective. Vocabulary building is a lifelong endeavor that extends beyond formal education. It involves continuous learning and practice, adapting to new contexts and evolving language use. For instance, professional and academic environments often introduce specialized vocabulary, requiring ongoing learning and adaptation. Similarly, personal interests and hobbies may also lead to the acquisition of domain-specific terms and expressions.

Effective vocabulary building not only improves language skills but also boosts confidence in communication. A well-developed vocabulary allows individuals to articulate ideas more precisely, engage in more meaningful conversations, and understand complex texts with greater ease. It also enhances critical thinking and analytical skills, as individuals with a rich vocabulary can better comprehend and evaluate diverse information. In summary, vocabulary building is a fundamental aspect of language development that involves exposure, active learning, and practical usage of words. Techniques such as reading, annotating, using vocabulary lists and flashcards, playing word games, and understanding word components contribute to expanding one's vocabulary. Engaging in contextual practice and immersive experiences further enhances vocabulary acquisition and retention. A rich vocabulary facilitates clearer expression, deeper comprehension, and effective communication, making it an essential component of personal and professional growth.

6.1 Synonyms and Antonyms

Synonyms and antonyms are crucial elements of vocabulary building, enhancing language skills by enabling more precise and varied expression. Synonyms are words with similar meanings, while antonyms are words with opposite meanings. Mastering the use of synonyms and antonyms not only enriches one's vocabulary but also improves communication, making it more dynamic and engaging. This chapter on vocabulary building delves into the significance, usage, and benefits of synonyms and antonyms. Synonyms are words that have the same or nearly the same meaning as another word. They are invaluable for avoiding repetition and making language more interesting and expressive. For example, the word "happy" has several synonyms, such as "joyful," "elated," "content," and "cheerful."

Using synonyms allows writers and speakers to add variety to their language, ensuring that their message remains engaging and clear. Instead of repeatedly using the word "happy," one might say, "She was joyful about her promotion," or "He felt content with his accomplishments." This variety in word choice keeps the audience interested and helps to convey subtle nuances in meaning. In addition to enhancing variety, synonyms can help in achieving the desired tone and precision in communication. For instance, while "happy" and "content" are similar, "elated" conveys a stronger sense of joy, and "cheerful" suggests a more outward expression of happiness. By choosing the most appropriate synonym, a writer can convey the exact emotion or level of intensity intended. This skill is particularly important in creative writing, persuasive writing, and any context where the tone is crucial. Antonyms, on the other hand, are words with opposite meanings.

They are essential for contrasting ideas and highlighting differences. For instance, the antonym of "happy" is "sad," and the opposite of "content" is "discontent" or "unhappy." Using antonyms allows writers and speakers to emphasize contrasts and make their points more effectively. For example, saying, "She was happy, but he was sad," immediately highlights the difference in their emotional states. Antonyms are also useful in argumentation and debate, where presenting opposing ideas can strengthen one's position by clearly delineating differences. Understanding and using antonyms can also enhance comprehension and critical thinking. When learning new vocabulary, recognizing the antonyms helps to solidify the meanings of words. For instance, knowing that "generous" is the opposite of "stingy" provides a clearer understanding of both words.

This dual approach to learning vocabulary—through synonyms and antonyms—ensures a deeper and more comprehensive grasp of the language. Moreover, the ability to use synonyms and antonyms effectively is a key component of language proficiency exams and standardized tests. These tests often include sections that assess vocabulary knowledge, and being adept at identifying and using synonyms and antonyms can significantly improve test scores. For students and professionals alike, a strong command of these elements is crucial for success in both academic and professional contexts. In summary, synonyms and antonyms are indispensable tools in vocabulary building. Synonyms enhance language by adding variety and allowing for more precise expression, while antonyms help in contrasting ideas and emphasizing differences. Mastery of these elements enriches communication, making it more effective, engaging, and nuanced. Whether in writing or speaking, the strategic use of synonyms and antonyms elevates the quality of language, facilitating clearer and more impactful expression. As learners expand their vocabulary through the study of synonyms and antonyms, they not only improve their language skills but also their ability to think critically and articulate their thoughts with greater accuracy and depth.

6.2 Homophones and Homonyms

Homophones and homonyms are fascinating aspects of the English language that often pose challenges but also offer opportunities for enriching vocabulary and enhancing communication skills. Homophones are words that sound the same but have different meanings and spellings, while homonyms are words that sound the same and may be spelled the same but have different meanings. Understanding these elements is crucial for mastering language nuances and avoiding common pitfalls in writing and speaking. This chapter on vocabulary building explores the significance, types, and usage of homophones and homonyms. Homophones are words that are pronounced identically but differ in meaning and spelling. Common examples include "flower" and "flour," "to," "two," and "too," and "right" and "write." Homophones are a rich source of puns and wordplay, making them valuable in creative writing and poetry.

However, they also require careful attention to context to avoid confusion. For instance, "He read the book," and "He red the book" would lead to different interpretations, but because "read" and "red" are homophones, they sound the same. Proper use of homophones ensures clarity and precision in communication, preventing misunderstandings that can arise from their similar sounds. Homophones are particularly challenging for learners of English and can often lead to spelling errors and misinterpretation.

For example, confusing "there," "their," and "they're" can change the meaning of a sentence entirely. "There" refers to a place, "their" denotes possession, and "they're" is a contraction of "they are." Understanding and correctly using homophones requires not only knowledge of their meanings but also practice in distinguishing them within context. Exercises that focus on sentence construction and context clues can help learners master homophones and enhance their overall language proficiency. Homonyms, on the other hand, include words that are both pronounced the same and often spelled the same, but have different meanings. Examples include "bat" (the flying mammal) and "bat" (the equipment used in sports), "bank" (the side of a river) and "bank" (a financial institution), and "lead" (to guide) and "lead" (a type of metal, pronounced differently but spelled the same).

Homonyms add richness and complexity to the language, providing opportunities for creativity in writing. They are often used in literature to create double meanings and add depth to texts. The key to mastering homonyms is understanding context. The meaning of a homonym is usually clear when seen within a sentence or a broader context. For instance, "He will lead the team," versus "The pipe was made of lead." In spoken language, tone and emphasis can also help differentiate between meanings. Writers and speakers must pay attention to the surrounding words and the overall context to ensure their intended meaning is conveyed accurately. Homophones and homonyms can also be a source of humor and wit. Puns, which are jokes exploiting the different possible meanings of a word or words that sound alike but have different meanings, often rely on homophones and homonyms. For example, "I used to be a baker, but I couldn't make enough dough," plays on the homonyms "dough" (money) and "dough" (bread mixture).

This playfulness with language not only makes communication enjoyable but also stimulates creative thinking and engagement with the language. In addition to their role in humor, homophones and homonyms are essential for language learners. They provide a deeper understanding of vocabulary and encourage learners to pay closer attention to pronunciation, spelling, and meaning. Learning these words helps in developing better reading comprehension skills and more precise writing abilities. Educators often use lists and exercises focused on homophones and homonyms to reinforce these skills and improve students' overall language competence. In conclusion, homophones and homonyms are integral parts of the English language that enhance its richness and complexity. Homophones require careful attention to context to avoid confusion, while homonyms offer opportunities for creativity and depth in communication.

Mastering these elements is crucial for clear and effective communication, whether in writing or speaking. They challenge learners to pay close attention to context and pronunciation, thereby improving their overall language skills. By understanding and correctly using homophones and homonyms, individuals can enrich their vocabulary, avoid common errors, and enjoy the playful and creative aspects of the English language.

6.3 Prefixes and Suffixes

Prefixes and suffixes are essential components of English vocabulary that significantly contribute to word formation, understanding, and enhancement of language skills. They are types of affixes—prefixes appear at the beginning of a word, and suffixes at the end—altering the meaning, function, or grammatical category of the base word to which they are attached. Mastery of prefixes and suffixes is crucial for vocabulary building, reading comprehension, and effective communication. Prefixes are affixes added to the beginning of a base word to modify its meaning. They often indicate negation, direction, time, degree, or manner. Common prefixes include "un-," "re-," "pre-," "mis-," and "dis-." For example, adding the prefix "un-" to the word "happy" forms "unhappy," indicating a negative or opposite meaning. Similarly, "re-" added to "write" forms "rewrite," suggesting repetition or doing something again. Prefixes can significantly expand one's vocabulary by allowing the formation of new words from familiar base words.

Understanding the meaning of a prefix can help in deducing the meaning of unfamiliar words. For instance, knowing that "pre-" means "before" can help one understand that "preview" means to view something before it is officially shown or released. This knowledge is particularly useful in academic and technical contexts where complex terminology is often used. Suffixes, on the other hand, are added to the end of a base word and often change its grammatical function. They can turn nouns into adjectives, adjectives into nouns, verbs into nouns, and so forth. Common suffixes include "-ness," "-able," "-ly," "-er," and "-tion." For instance, adding "-ness" to "happy" forms "happiness," turning an adjective into a noun. Similarly, "-ly" added to "quick" forms "quickly," transforming an adjective into an adverb. Suffixes also play a crucial role in verb conjugation and tense formation. For example, adding "-ed" to a verb typically forms the past tense, as in "talk" becoming "talked." Understanding suffixes is essential for mastering English grammar and syntax, as they often indicate the function of a word within a sentence and its relationship to other words.

The study of prefixes and suffixes not only aids in vocabulary expansion but also enhances spelling and pronunciation skills. Recognizing common affixes helps learners identify word patterns and understand how words are constructed. This understanding can lead to more accurate spelling and pronunciation, as learners become familiar with the typical ways in which words are modified. In addition to vocabulary expansion, prefixes and suffixes contribute to more precise and expressive language use. They allow for the creation of nuanced meanings and variations of base words, enabling more detailed and specific communication. For example, the word "cycle" can be modified with the prefix "bi-" to form "bicycle," indicating two wheels, or with the prefix "tri-" to form "tricycle," indicating three wheels. These modifications provide clarity and specificity in description and expression. Moreover, a strong grasp of prefixes and suffixes is invaluable for academic and professional success. Many specialized terms in fields such as medicine, law, science, and technology are formed using these affixes.

For instance, in medical terminology, the prefix "hyper-" means "over" or "excessive," as in "hypertension" (high blood pressure), while the suffix "-itis" indicates inflammation, as in "arthritis" (inflammation of the joints). Understanding these components can greatly aid in comprehending and retaining complex terminology. In educational settings, teaching prefixes and suffixes is a key strategy for improving reading comprehension and literacy skills. By breaking down words into their component parts, students can better understand and remember their meanings. This approach also helps in deciphering unfamiliar words, leading to greater confidence and proficiency in reading and writing. In conclusion, prefixes and suffixes are vital tools in the English language that facilitate word formation, enhance vocabulary, and improve comprehension and communication skills. Prefixes modify the meaning of base words, while suffixes often change their grammatical function, allowing for the creation of a wide variety of words and expressions. Mastery of these affixes is essential for academic success, professional communication, and overall language proficiency. By understanding and effectively using prefixes and suffixes, individuals can expand their vocabulary, improve their spelling and pronunciation, and communicate with greater clarity and precision.

CHAPTER - 7

VERB TENSES AND FORMS

7. Introduction of Tenses

Verb tense and form are fundamental elements of grammar that play a crucial role in conveying the timing, duration, and nature of actions or states described in sentences. Mastering verb tense and form is essential for clear and precise communication, as it allows speakers and writers to accurately depict when events occur and how they relate to each other. Verb tense refers to the grammatical category that locates a situation in time, indicating when an action takes place. English verbs are categorized into three primary tenses: past, present, and future. Each tense has its own set of forms that help convey different aspects of time. The present tense describes actions occurring currently or habitual actions. It is typically used for statements about facts or general truths, such as "She writes articles" or "Water boils at 100 degrees Celsius." In English, the present tense has simple, progressive, perfect, and perfect progressive forms.

The simple present is used for routine actions or general truths. The present progressive (e.g., "She is writing") indicates an ongoing action happening at the moment of speaking. The present perfect (e.g., "She has written") denotes an action completed at some indefinite time in the past with relevance to the present. The present perfect progressive (e.g., "She has been writing") shows an ongoing action that started in the past and continues into the present. The past tense describes actions that have already happened. It can be divided into the simple past, past progressive, past perfect, and past perfect progressive. The simple past is used for actions that were completed in the past, such as "She wrote the letter." The past progressive (e.g., "She was writing") describes an ongoing action that was happening at a specific point in the past.

The past perfect (e.g., "She had written") indicates that an action was completed before another action in the past. The past perfect progressive (e.g., "She had been writing") shows that an action was ongoing before another past action, emphasizing the duration of the activity. The future tense refers to actions that will occur after the present time. It includes the simple future, future progressive, future perfect, and future perfect progressive forms. The simple future (e.g., "She will write") indicates an action that will happen in the future. The future progressive (e.g., "She will be writing") describes an ongoing action that will be happening at a specific time in the future. The future perfect (e.g., "She will have written") refers to an action that will be completed before a specified future time.

The future perfect progressive (e.g., "She will have been writing") shows that an action will be ongoing up until a certain future point, focusing on the duration of the action. Verb form encompasses not only tense but also aspect, voice, and mood, which further refine the meaning of verbs. Aspect indicates the nature of the action in relation to time. The simple aspect describes actions without specifying their duration or completion. The progressive aspect shows ongoing actions or events, while the perfect aspect indicates actions that are completed or have relevance to other times. The perfect progressive aspect combines the perfect and progressive aspects, highlighting actions that were ongoing and have continued up to the present or into the future. Voice in verbs can be either active or passive. In the active voice, the subject performs the action, as in "The chef prepared the meal." In the passive voice, the subject receives the action, as in "The meal was prepared by the chef." Understanding the difference between active and passive voice helps in choosing the most effective way to present information and emphasizes different aspects of a sentence.

Mood expresses the speaker's attitude toward the action or state described by the verb. English has three primary moods: indicative, imperative, and subjunctive. The indicative mood is used for statements of fact or questions, such as "She writes every day." The imperative mood gives commands or requests, such as "Write the report." The subjunctive mood is used to express wishes, hypotheticals, or conditions contrary to fact, such as "If she were here, she would write the letter." Understanding and correctly using verb tense and form are vital for clear communication. Accurate verb tenses convey the timing of actions, helping listeners and readers understand when events occur and how they relate to one another. Correct verb forms provide additional information about the nature and duration of actions, adding depth and precision to language. Mastery of these elements enhances both written and spoken communication, allowing for more effective expression and comprehension of ideas.

7.1 Present, Past, and Future Tenses

In the realm of verb tenses, understanding the distinctions between the present, past, and future tenses is crucial for conveying time and clarity in writing and speech. These tenses help to specify when an action occurs, making communication more precise and coherent. This chapter on verb tenses explores the present, past, and future tenses in detail, providing a comprehensive guide to their usage and forms.

7.1.1 Present Tense

The present tense is used to describe actions or states that are currently happening, habitual actions, or general truths. It is the most immediate and direct tense, allowing speakers and writers to convey real-time events or ongoing situations. The present tense is divided into several forms:

- **Simple Present Tense**: This form is used to express habitual actions, general truths, and fixed arrangements. For example, "She writes a letter every week" indicates a regular action, while "Water boils at 100°C" reflects a general truth. The simple present tense is formed by using the base form of the verb for most subjects (I, you, we, they) and adding an "s" or "es" for third-person singular subjects (he, she, it).

- **Present Continuous Tense**: This form describes actions that are happening at the moment of speaking. It is formed using the auxiliary verb "am/is/are" followed by the present participle (verb + -ing). For example, "She is writing a letter right now" shows that the action is ongoing.

- **Present Perfect Tense**: This form indicates actions that have been completed at some point before now but have relevance to the present. It is formed using "has/have" followed by the past participle of the verb. For example, "They have finished their homework" implies that the action is completed but affects the present situation.

- **Present Perfect Continuous Tense**: This tense highlights actions that started in the past and are still continuing or have recently stopped, with emphasis on the duration. It is formed using "has/have been" followed by the present participle. For instance, "She has been writing for two hours" shows the ongoing nature of the action.

7.1.2 Past Tense

The past tense is used to describe actions or states that occurred and were completed at a specific time in the past. It allows for reflection on events that are no longer ongoing. The past tense is also divided into several forms:

- **Simple Past Tense**: This form describes actions that were completed at a definite time in the past. It is typically formed by adding "-ed" to regular verbs (e.g., "walked," "jumped") or using the irregular forms of verbs (e.g., "went" from "go"). For example, "She wrote a letter yesterday" indicates that the action was completed in the past.

- **Past Continuous Tense**: This form is used to describe actions that were in progress at a particular point in the past. It is formed using "was/were" followed by the present participle. For example, "She was writing a letter when I called her" shows that the action was ongoing at the time of another event.

- **Past Perfect Tense**: This tense indicates that an action was completed before another action or point in the past. It is formed using "had" followed by the past participle. For example, "She had written the letter before the meeting started" shows that the action was completed prior to another past event.

- **Past Perfect Continuous Tense**: This form emphasizes the duration of an action that was ongoing up to a specific point in the past. It is formed using "had been" followed by the present participle. For instance, "She had been writing for two hours when the meeting started" highlights the ongoing nature of the action before another past event.

7.1.3 Future Tense

The future tense is used to describe actions or states that will occur after the present moment. It helps to express plans, predictions, and intentions. The future tense is divided into several forms:

- **Simple Future Tense:** This form describes actions that will happen at a future time. It is formed using "will" followed by the base form of the verb. For example, "She will write a letter tomorrow" indicates a future action.

- **Future Continuous Tense**: This tense describes actions that will be in progress at a specific future time. It is formed using "will be" followed by the present participle. For example, "She will be writing a letter at 8 PM" shows that the action will be ongoing at a future time.

- **Future Perfect Tense**: This form indicates that an action will be completed before a specific future time or event. It is formed using "will have" followed by the past participle. For instance, "She will have written the letter by the time the meeting starts" shows that the action will be completed before another future event.

- **Future Perfect Continuous Tense**: This tense highlights the duration of an action that will be ongoing up to a specific future point. It is formed using "will have been" followed by the present participle. For example, "She will have been writing for two hours by the time the meeting starts" emphasizes the ongoing nature of the action before another future event.

Understanding and mastering these tenses is crucial for effective communication. They allow speakers and writers to place actions in time, whether they are occurring now, have already occurred, or will occur in the future. By accurately using present, past, and future tenses, individuals can convey clear and precise messages, enhancing both written and spoken communication.

7.2 Perfect and Progressive Tenses

Understanding perfect and progressive tenses is crucial for mastering the subtleties of English grammar and conveying precise time frames and actions. These tenses help to describe not only the timing of actions but also their completion, duration, and ongoing nature. This section delves into the perfect and progressive tenses, exploring their forms, uses, and distinctions.

7.2.1 Perfect Tenses

Perfect tenses are used to express actions that are completed relative to another time or event. They provide insight into the relationship between different times and the state of completion of actions. There are three primary perfect tenses: the present perfect, the past perfect, and the future perfect.

1. Present Perfect Tense

The present perfect tense describes actions that occurred at an unspecified time before now and have relevance to the present moment. It can also describe actions that started in the past and continue into the present. The form is created using the auxiliary verbs "has" or "have" followed by the past participle of the main verb. For example:

- "She has finished her homework." (The action of finishing homework is completed, and it affects the present situation.)
- "They have lived here for five years." (They started living here

five years ago and are still living here.)

- The present perfect tense emphasizes the result or impact of the action on the present, rather than when the action occurred.

2. Past Perfect Tense

The past perfect tense is used to describe an action that was completed before another action or time in the past. It is formed with "had" followed by the past participle of the main verb. For instance:

- "She had already left when I arrived." (Her departure was completed before my arrival.)

- "By the time the movie started, they had bought their tickets." (The buying of tickets was completed before the movie started.)

- The past perfect tense helps to clarify the sequence of past events, providing a clear understanding of what happened first

3. Future Perfect Tense

The future perfect tense indicates that an action will be completed before a specified point in the future. It is constructed using "will have" followed by the past participle of the verb. Examples include:

- "By next year, I will have graduated from college." (The action of graduating will be completed before next year.)

- "She will have finished the report by the time the meeting starts." (The report will be completed before the meeting begins.)

- This tense helps to project into the future and express actions that will be completed by a certain future moment.

7.2.2 Progressive Tenses

Progressive tenses, also known as continuous tenses, describe actions that are ongoing or in progress at a specific time. They focus on the duration or ongoing nature of the action. There are three main progressive tenses: the present progressive, the past progressive, and the future progressive.

1. Present Progressive Tense

The present progressive tense describes actions that are currently happening at the moment of speaking. It is formed using the verb "to be" (am/is/are) followed by the present participle (verb + -ing). For example:

2. Past Progressive Tense

The past progressive tense describes actions that were ongoing at a particular point in the past. It is created using "was/were" followed by the present participle. Examples include:

3. Future Progressive Tense

The future progressive tense describes actions that will be ongoing at a specific point in the future. It is formed using "will be" followed by the present participle for instance.

7.2.3 Combining Perfect and Progressive Tenses

Perfect and progressive tenses can be combined to describe actions that are both completed and ongoing. For example:

- Present Perfect Progressive Tense: "She has been working on her project all day." (The action of working started in the past, is ongoing, and has relevance to the present.)

- Past Perfect Progressive Tense: "They had been waiting for hours when the train finally arrived." (The action of waiting was ongoing up to a specific point in the past.)

- Future Perfect Progressive Tense: "By next year, she will have been teaching for 20 years." (The action of teaching will have been ongoing for a period up to a specific future point.)

In conclusion, perfect and progressive tenses provide nuanced ways to express actions relative to time. Perfect tenses focus on the completion and relevance of actions, while progressive tenses emphasize ongoing activity. Mastery of these tenses enhances the ability to communicate with precision and clarity, allowing for detailed descriptions of actions in various time frames.

7.3 Irregular Verbs

Irregular verbs are an essential aspect of English grammar, distinguished by their unique and non-standard patterns of conjugation. Unlike regular verbs, which follow a predictable pattern when forming past tenses and past participles, irregular verbs do not adhere to these typical rules, making them more challenging to learn and use correctly. This section explores the nature of irregular verbs, their categories, and strategies for mastering them.

- **Understanding Irregular Verbs**

In English, regular verbs form their past tense and past participle by adding "-ed" to the base form (e.g., "walk" becomes "walked"). Irregular verbs, however, do not follow this rule and instead have varied and often unpredictable changes in their forms. For instance, the verb "go" becomes "went" in the past tense and "gone" in the past participle, which deviates from the regular pattern.

Irregular verbs are categorized based on their conjugation patterns. Here are the main types:

1. **Completely Irregular Verbs** - These verbs do not follow any specific pattern and each verb may have a unique set of past tense and past participle forms. Examples include:

2. **Verbs with Vowel Changes**- Some irregular verbs undergo changes in the vowel sounds in their past tense and past participle forms.

3. **Verbs with Same Form**- Certain irregular verbs have the same form for the base, past tense, and past participle. These verbs often remain unchanged across different tenses.

4. **Mixed Patterns**- Some irregular verbs exhibit mixed patterns, combining elements from different types of irregularities.

7.4 Strategies for Mastery

1. Memorization

One of the most effective strategies for mastering irregular verbs is to memorize their forms. Flashcards, lists, and repetitive practice can help reinforce these verbs. Creating mnemonic devices or associations can also aid in remembering the irregular forms.

2. Practice in Context

Using irregular verbs in sentences and real-life contexts helps solidify understanding and usage. Writing sentences, paragraphs, or even short stories using these verbs can reinforce their correct forms and usage.

3. Regular Review

Regular review and practice of irregular verbs are essential for retention. Incorporating these verbs into daily practice routines, quizzes, and exercises ensures that their forms remain fresh in memory.

4. Learning Patterns

While irregular verbs do not follow standard rules, some patterns do exist. For example, verbs like "sing," "ring," and "drink" share similar vowel changes. Identifying and learning these patterns can make it easier to remember and use irregular verbs correctly.

5. Exposure

Reading and listening to a wide range of English texts, including literature, articles, and conversations, exposes learners to irregular verbs in context. This exposure helps reinforce their correct usage and understanding.

Conclusion

Irregular verbs are a unique and important aspect of English grammar, characterized by their non-standard conjugation patterns. Understanding and mastering these verbs is essential for effective communication, as they frequently appear in both written and spoken English. By employing strategies such as memorization, contextual practice, regular review, learning patterns, and exposure, learners can gain proficiency with irregular verbs and enhance their overall language skills. Mastery of irregular verbs not only contributes to grammatical accuracy but also improves fluency and confidence in using the English language.

CHAPTER - 8

ACTIVE AND PASSIVE VOICE

8 Introduction of voice

Active and passive voice are two fundamental ways to structure sentences, each offering a different focus and impact on communication. Understanding the distinction between these voices is crucial for effective writing and speaking, as it influences how information is presented and perceived. In the active voice, the subject of the sentence performs the action expressed by the verb. This structure is straightforward and direct, making it the preferred choice for clarity and emphasis in most situations. For example, in the sentence "The teacher explained the lesson," the subject "the teacher" is actively performing the action of explaining, and the object "the lesson" is receiving the action.

The active voice typically follows a clear pattern: subject-verb-object, which facilitates readability and keeps the focus on who is doing what. This direct approach is particularly useful in instructional or persuasive writing, where clear and compelling communication is essential. On the other hand, the passive voice reverses this structure by making the object of the action the subject of the sentence. In passive constructions, the action is performed upon the subject rather than by it. For example, the sentence "The lesson was explained by the teacher" shifts the focus from the doer of the action to the recipient of the action. Here, "the lesson" becomes the subject, and "was explained" is the passive verb phrase. The agent performing the action, "the teacher," can either be included or omitted from the sentence, depending on whether their identity is relevant. The passive voice often follows a pattern of object-verb-subject, and the emphasis is placed on the action or the recipient rather than the doer. The choice between active and passive voice affects the emphasis and clarity of a sentence. The active voice is generally more dynamic and engaging, making it ideal for most writing contexts, including narratives, reports, and persuasive texts. It clearly identifies the agent of the action and provides a more vigorous and straightforward account of events. For example, "The chef prepared a gourmet meal" highlights the chef's role in the action and underscores their contribution to the outcome. Conversely, the passive voice can be advantageous in situations where the focus should be on the action itself or when the doer of the action is unknown or less important.

In scientific or technical writing, the passive voice is frequently used to emphasize the process or results rather than the researcher. For instance, "The experiment was conducted under controlled conditions" focuses on the procedure rather than on who performed it. This use of passive voice can also help maintain an objective tone and shift the reader's attention to the work rather than the individual conducting it. However, overuse of the passive voice can lead to vague or convoluted sentences. It may obscure who is responsible for the action and create ambiguity. For example, "Mistakes were made" fails to specify who made the mistakes, which can detract from accountability and clarity. In such cases, the passive voice can weaken the impact of the writing and diminish its effectiveness.

Therefore, while the passive voice has its place, it is important to use it judiciously and ensure that the sentence remains clear and purposeful. In summary, the active and passive voices serve different functions in writing and speaking. The active voice is direct and clear, emphasizing the subject and making the action prominent. It is generally preferred for its straightforwardness and effectiveness in most contexts. The passive voice, while sometimes necessary for shifting focus or maintaining objectivity, should be used carefully to avoid ambiguity and maintain clarity. Mastery of both voices allows writers and speakers to choose the most appropriate structure for their message, enhancing communication and ensuring that the intended emphasis is achieved.

8.1 Understanding Active Voice

Understanding the active voice is fundamental to mastering English sentence structure and ensuring clear, direct communication. The active voice is a grammatical structure where the subject of the sentence performs the action expressed by the verb. This contrasts with the passive voice, where the subject receives the action. By using the active voice, writers and speakers can create sentences that are typically more engaging, straightforward, and dynamic.

- **What is Active Voice?**

In the active voice, the subject of the sentence is the doer of the action. The basic structure of an active voice sentence is:

- Subject + Verb + Object

For example:

1. "The teacher (subject) explains (verb) the lesson (object)."
2. "The cat (subject) chased (verb) the mouse (object)."

In these examples, the subject is clearly performing the action of the verb on the object. This structure makes it easy for readers and listeners to follow who is doing what, which helps in maintaining clarity and focus.

1. Characteristics of Active Voice

1. Clarity and Directness: Active voice sentences are generally more straightforward and easier to understand. They present information in a direct manner, which helps in avoiding ambiguity. For instance, "The chef cooked the meal" is clearer than "The meal was cooked by the chef."

2. Engagement: Active voice often makes writing more engaging and lively. It tends to create a stronger connection between the subject and the action, which can make sentences more compelling. For example, "The team won the championship" is more immediate and engaging than "The championship was won by the team."

3. Conciseness: Active voice sentences are typically more concise. They avoid unnecessary words that might come with passive constructions, leading to more efficient communication. For instance, "She wrote the report" is shorter and more direct than "The report was written by her."

2. Forming Active Voice Sentences

To construct sentences in the active voice, follow these steps:

1. **Identify the Subject**: Determine who or what is performing the action. In the sentence "The dog barked," "The dog" is the subject performing the action.

2. **Determine the Verb**: Identify the action being performed by the subject. In "The dog barked," "barked" is the verb.

3. **Identify the Object**: Determine what or whom the action is being performed on, if applicable. In "The dog chased the cat," "the

cat" is the object receiving the action of chasing.

4. **Assemble the Sentence**: Combine the subject, verb, and object in the active voice structure. For example, "The dog (subject) chased (verb) the cat (object)."

3. Examples and Application

Here are some additional examples of active voice sentences across different contexts:

- Personal Context: "Sarah (subject) writes (verb) letters (object) every day."
- Professional Context: "The manager (subject) approved (verb) the new policy (object)."
- Academic Context: "The scientist (subject) conducted (verb) the experiment (object)."

In each example, the subject is directly performing the action, creating a clear and effective sentence structure.

4. Benefits of Using Active Voice

1. Enhanced Readability: Active voice contributes to easier and more engaging reading. Readers can quickly identify who is doing what, which improves comprehension and retention.

2. Strong Communication: By making sentences more direct, active voice strengthens the message and ensures that the intended meaning is communicated clearly.

3. Effective Writing: Active voice often leads to more dynamic and impactful writing. It helps convey actions and events with greater immediacy and energy.

5. When to Use Active Voice

While active voice is often preferable for clarity and engagement, there are times when the passive voice might be more appropriate, such as when the focus needs to be on the action or the receiver of the action rather than the doer. For instance, in scientific writing or formal reports, the passive voice can emphasize the action over the researcher. However, in most cases, especially in everyday communication and narrative writing, the active voice is preferred for its straightforwardness and effectiveness.

Conclusion

Understanding and using the active voice is crucial for clear and impactful communication in English. It ensures that sentences are direct, engaging, and easy to understand by placing the subject at the forefront of the action. By mastering active voice constructions, writers and speakers can enhance their ability to convey information effectively and maintain reader or listener interest. Active voice not only simplifies sentence structure but also contributes to more dynamic and persuasive communication, making it a fundamental aspect of effective writing and speaking.

8.2 Understanding Passive Voice

Understanding the passive voice is crucial for mastering the nuances of English grammar and enhancing your ability to convey information in varied contexts. The passive voice is a grammatical construction where the focus is on the action or the recipient of the action, rather than on who or what is performing the action. This contrasts with the active voice, where the subject performs the action. The passive voice is used to shift emphasis, highlight the receiver of the action, or when the doer is unknown or irrelevant.

- **What is Passive Voice?**

In the passive voice, the subject of the sentence is the recipient of the action rather than the performer. The typical structure of a passive voice sentence is:

- Subject + Form of "to be" + Past Participle + (Optional: by + Agent)

For example:

1. "The cake (subject) was baked (form of "to be" + past participle) by Mary (agent)."

2. "The report (subject) is being reviewed (form of "to be" + present participle) by the manager (agent)."

In these examples, the focus is on the action or the receiver of the action, and the doer (if mentioned) appears in a prepositional phrase beginning with "by."

1. Characteristics of Passive Voice

1. **Focus on the Action or Recipient**: The passive voice emphasizes the action or the recipient of the action rather than the doer. For example, "The book was read by millions" highlights the book and the fact that it was read, rather than focusing on who read it.

2. **Agent May be Omitted**: In many passive constructions, the agent (the one performing the action) is omitted if it is unknown or not important. For instance, "The letter was sent" does not specify who sent the letter, focusing instead on the fact that the letter was sent.

3. **Use of Auxiliary** Verbs: The passive voice relies on auxiliary verbs ("to be" in various forms) and the past participle of the main verb. For example, "The car is repaired" uses "is" (a form of "to be") and "repaired" (past participle).

2. Forming Passive Voice Sentences

To construct a passive voice sentence, follow these steps:

1. Identify the Object: Determine the object of the action in the

active voice sentence. For instance, in "The chef cooked the meal," the object is "the meal."

2. Identify the Form of "to be": Choose the correct form of the verb "to be" based on the tense of the original active sentence. For example, "The chef cooked the meal" (past tense) would use "was" or "were" in the passive voice.

3. Use the Past Participle: Apply the past participle of the main verb. For "cooked," the past participle is also "cooked."

4. Rearrange the Sentence: Place the object as the subject, followed by the appropriate form of "to be," the past participle, and optionally the original subject (agent) in a prepositional phrase with "by."

3. Examples of Passive Voice

Here are several examples of how different tenses are used in the passive voice:

1. Present Simple Passive:

a. Active: "The company produces high-quality products."

b. Passive: "High-quality products are produced by the company."

2. Past Simple Passive:

a. Active: "The artist painted the mural."

b. Passive: "The mural was painted by the artist."

3. Present Continuous Passive:

a. Active: "The team is developing a new software."

b. Passive: "A new software is being developed by the team."

4. Past Continuous Passive:

a. Active: "The students were taking the exam."

b. Passive: "The exam was being taken by the students."

5. Future Simple Passive:

a. Active: "The company will launch the new product."

b. Passive: "The new product will be launched by the company."

6. Present Perfect Passive:

a. Active: "The chef has prepared the meal."

b. Passive: "The meal has been prepared by the chef."

4. When to Use Passive Voice

• When the Doer is Unknown or Unimportant: The passive voice is useful when the identity of the doer is not known or is irrelevant. For instance, "The house was built in 1920" focuses on the house and its history, rather than who built it.

• To Emphasize the Action or Result: If the action or result is more important than the performer, the passive voice highlights the action itself. For example, "The final report will be submitted tomorrow" emphasizes the submission of the report rather than who will submit it.

• In Formal or Scientific Writing: Passive voice is often used in formal writing, scientific reports, and academic papers to focus on processes and results rather than individual actions. For example, "The experiment was conducted to test the hypothesis" shifts the focus to the experiment rather than the researcher.

Conclusion

Understanding and using the passive voice is crucial for effective communication in English. It allows speakers and writers to shift emphasis, highlight different aspects of an action, and handle situations where the doer is unknown or irrelevant. By mastering passive voice constructions, you can enhance your ability to present information in varied and nuanced ways, adapting your communication style to fit different contexts and purposes. Whether aiming for clarity, formality, or emphasis, the passive voice is a valuable tool in the arsenal of English grammar.

8.3 Converting Between Voices

Converting between active and passive voice is an essential skill in mastering English grammar, as it allows for greater flexibility in expression and emphasis in writing and speaking. The process involves transforming a sentence from its active voice form, where the subject performs the action, to its passive voice form, where the subject receives the action. This can be useful for varying sentence structure, emphasizing different elements of a sentence, or focusing on different aspects of the action.

Conclusion

Mastering the conversion between active and passive voice is key to effective writing and communication. It allows for flexibility in focusing on different elements of a sentence, whether it's the doer of the action or the action itself. By understanding and applying these conversions, you can enhance your ability to craft clear, engaging, and varied sentences, adapting your writing style to suit different contexts and purposes.

CHAPTER - 9

DIRECT AND INDIRECT SPEECH

9   Introduction of Speech

Direct and indirect speech are two ways of reporting or conveying what someone has said, each serving distinct purposes in communication. Understanding the differences between these two forms is crucial for accurate and effective expression in both written and spoken language. Direct speech involves quoting the exact words spoken by someone, often enclosed in quotation marks. This method preserves the speaker's original wording, tone, and nuances, providing a precise and vivid account of the dialogue. For example, if a character says, "I am going to the store," using direct speech in a narrative or conversation clearly captures their exact words and intent.

Direct speech is commonly used in literature, journalism, and everyday conversation to convey the speaker's voice and emotions authentically. It adds immediacy and realism to the dialogue, allowing the audience to experience the speaker's expression directly. When using direct speech, punctuation is crucial: quotation marks enclose the spoken words, and commas or periods typically precede the closing quotation marks, depending on the sentence structure. Indirect speech, also known as reported speech, involves paraphrasing or summarizing what someone has said without quoting their exact words. Instead of repeating the speaker's words verbatim, indirect speech conveys the meaning of the message in the reporter's own words. For instance, the sentence "She said that she was going to the store" translates the speaker's original message into indirect speech.

This method focuses on the essence of the communication rather than the exact phrasing, which can be useful for providing a concise overview of conversations or statements. Indirect speech often involves changes in pronouns, verb tenses, and word order to fit the context of the reporting sentence. For example, "I am going to the store" in direct speech becomes "She said that she was going to the store" in indirect speech, reflecting the shift in perspective and tense. Both direct and indirect speech have their advantages and applications. Direct speech is beneficial when the exact words of the speaker are important for capturing the authenticity and emotional impact of their message. It is particularly effective in creative writing, such as novels and plays, where character voices and dialogue are central to the narrative. It also enhances the immediacy of news reporting and interviews, allowing readers or listeners to engage directly with the speaker's statements.

Indirect speech, on the other hand, is useful for summarizing or integrating reported information into a larger context. It allows for smoother integration of quotes into the narrative or text, particularly in formal writing, academic papers, or reports where the focus is on the content rather than the exact phrasing. Indirect speech helps avoid the fragmentation that can occur with excessive use of direct quotes and maintains a cohesive flow in the writing. In summary, direct and indirect speech serve different purposes in communication. Direct speech quotes the exact words spoken, preserving the speaker's original voice and emotional tone, making it ideal for dialogue, creative writing, and immediate reporting. Indirect speech paraphrases the content, offering a concise and integrated summary, which is useful for formal writing and reporting. Mastery of both forms allows for versatile and effective expression, enhancing clarity and engagement in various contexts.

9.1 Definition and Examples

Direct and indirect speech are fundamental concepts in grammar that deal with how we report or convey someone else's words. Understanding these forms is essential for clear and accurate communication in both written and spoken English. Here's a detailed look at each, including definitions and examples:

9.1.1 Definition of Direct Speech

Direct Speech: Direct speech, also known as quoted speech, is a way of reporting someone's exact words. In direct speech, the speaker's exact words are enclosed in quotation marks and are presented as they were spoken. This form preserves the original wording, punctuation, and tone of the speaker's message. Structure: Introduction Clause + Quotation: "Quotation" (Introduction Clause).

Example:

- John said, "I will go to the store tomorrow."
- "Can you help me with this?" asked Maria.

In these examples, the speaker's exact words are enclosed in quotation marks, maintaining the original phrasing and punctuation.

9.1.2 Definition of Indirect Speech

Indirect Speech: Indirect speech, also known as reported speech, involves conveying the meaning of what someone said without quoting their exact words. Instead of using quotation marks, indirect speech often involves a reporting verb (such as said, told, asked) and a change in pronouns, verb tense, and sometimes word order. The focus is on the content of the message rather than the exact wording. Structure: Reporting Clause + Content Clause: Reporting Clause + That + Content Clause.

Example:

- John said that he would go to the store the next day.
- Maria asked if I could help her with that.

In these examples, the exact words are not quoted, but the message is conveyed through a reporting clause and a content clause.

9.2 Rules for Conversion

Understanding and mastering the rules for conversation is essential for effective communication and fostering meaningful relationships. These rules ensure that conversations are productive, respectful, and engaging. Here's a comprehensive guide on the fundamental rules for conversation:

1. Active Listening

Active Listening is the cornerstone of effective communication. It involves not just hearing the words but understanding and engaging with the speaker's message.

- Full Attention: Give your complete focus to the speaker. This means putting away distractions like phones and computers and maintaining eye contact.

- Acknowledge and Reflect: Show that you're listening by nodding, making small verbal acknowledgments ("I see," "That's interesting"), and reflecting on what has been said ("So, you're saying...").

- Ask Clarifying Questions: If something is unclear, ask questions to gain a deeper understanding ("Can you explain what you mean by...?").

2. Respectful Communication

Respectful Communication ensures that all participants in a conversation feel valued and heard.

- Avoid Interruptions: Allow the speaker to finish their thoughts before responding. Interrupting can come across as disrespectful and may derail the conversation.

- Polite Language: Use courteous language and expressions, such as "please," "thank you," and "sorry," where appropriate. This fosters a positive conversational environment.

- Respect Different Viewpoints: Even if you disagree, acknowledge the validity of the other person's perspective and express your own views respectfully.

3. Clear and Concise Expression

Clear and Concise Expression helps to prevent misunderstandings and keeps the conversation focused.

- Be Direct: Clearly state your points without ambiguity or unnecessary complexity. Direct communication helps avoid confusion.

- Use Simple Language: Choose words and phrases that are easy to understand, avoiding jargon or overly complex terminology unless it's appropriate for the context.

- Stick to the Topic: Keep the discussion relevant to the subject at hand to avoid straying into unrelated areas.

4. Appropriate Body Language

Appropriate Body Language supports and enhances verbal communication through non-verbal cues.

- Maintain Eye Contact: This shows engagement and sincerity. However, be mindful of cultural differences in eye contact norms.

- Be Conscious of Gestures: Use gestures to emphasize points, but avoid overusing them or using gestures that might be misinterpreted.

- Observe Others' Non-Verbal Cues: Pay attention to the body language of others to gauge their reactions and adjust your communication style accordingly.

5. Turn-Taking

Turn-Taking is the practice of allowing each participant in the conversation a chance to speak without dominating the discussion.

- Wait Your Turn: Let others finish speaking before you begin. This shows respect for their contributions and helps maintain a smooth flow of conversation.

- Encourage Others to Speak: Invite quieter participants to share their thoughts, which can enrich the conversation and provide diverse perspectives.

- Handle Pauses Gracefully: Use pauses to allow others time to respond and to reflect on the conversation's content.

6. Empathy and Understanding

Empathy and Understanding involve recognizing and acknowledging the feelings and viewpoints of others.

- Show Empathy: Express understanding and compassion for others' emotions and experiences ("I can imagine how that must feel...").

- Ask Open-Ended Questions: Encourage more in-depth responses and greater sharing of thoughts and feelings ("What's your opinion on...?").

7. Constructive Feedback

Constructive Feedback is aimed at helping others improve and is delivered in a supportive manner.

- Be Specific: Provide clear, actionable feedback rather than vague comments ("Your presentation would benefit from more detailed data").

- Balance Positive and Negative: Offer praise for what was done well along with suggestions for improvement to make feedback more balanced and encouraging.

8. Avoiding Common Pitfalls

Avoiding Common Pitfalls involves steering clear of behaviors that can disrupt or harm the conversation.

- Avoid Gossip: Refrain from discussing individuals who are not present or speaking about sensitive topics that could cause discomfort.

- Manage Emotions: Keep your emotions in check to ensure they don't negatively impact the conversation or lead to conflict.

- Mind Your Tone: Use a tone that reflects your intended message. Ensure it is appropriate for the context and does not come across as sarcastic or aggressive.

9. Cultural Sensitivity

Cultural Sensitivity involves being aware of and respectful toward cultural differences in communication styles.

- Understand Cultural Norms: Recognize that communication practices may vary between cultures. What is considered polite or appropriate in one culture may differ in another.

- Adapt Your Communication: Adjust your language, tone, and behavior to accommodate the cultural context of your conversation partners.

10. Effective Questioning

Effective Questioning helps guide and enhance the conversation.

- Use Clarifying Questions: When needed, ask questions to better understand what has been said ("Could you elaborate on...?").

- Encourage Dialogue: Ask questions that invite deeper discussion and exploration of ideas ("What are your thoughts on this issue?").

Conclusion

Mastering the rules of conversation is vital for fostering effective and respectful communication. By actively listening, communicating respectfully, and employing clear expression, you contribute to a productive dialogue. Understanding and practicing these conversational rules not only enhances your ability to engage in meaningful discussions but also helps build stronger, more positive relationships in both personal and professional contexts.

CHAPTER - 10

CLAUSES AND PHRASES

10 Introduction of Clauses and Phrases

Clauses and phrases are essential components of sentence structure that help convey meaning and provide clarity in writing and speaking. Understanding how they function and differ is crucial for constructing well-organized and grammatically correct sentences. A clause is a group of words that contains both a subject and a predicate. Clauses can be classified into two main types: independent clauses and dependent clauses. An independent clause can stand alone as a complete sentence because it expresses a complete thought. For example, "She enjoys reading" is an independent clause. It has a subject ("She") and a predicate ("enjoys reading"), and it conveys a complete idea. On the other hand, a dependent clause (or subordinate clause) cannot stand alone as a complete sentence because it depends on an independent clause to provide a complete meaning.

For instance, "Although she enjoys reading" is a dependent clause. It introduces a condition but leaves the thought incomplete, requiring an independent clause to complete the meaning, such as "Although she enjoys reading, she rarely has time for it." Dependent clauses can further be categorized into adjective clauses, adverbial clauses, and noun clauses. Adjective clauses modify nouns or pronouns, providing more detail. For example, "The book that she lent me is fascinating" includes the adjective clause "that she lent me," which describes "the book." Adverbial clauses modify verbs, adjectives, or adverbs, often indicating time, reason, condition, or contrast.

For example, "She studied hard because she wanted to pass the exam" features the adverbial clause "because she wanted to pass the exam," explaining the reason for studying hard. Noun clauses function as nouns within a sentence. For instance, "What she said was surprising" includes the noun clause "What she said," which acts as the subject of the sentence. A phrase, on the other hand, is a group of related words that does not contain both a subject and a predicate. Phrases can serve different grammatical functions within a sentence and are classified into several types, including noun phrases, verb phrases, adjective phrases, and adverbial phrases. A noun phrase includes a noun and its modifiers, providing more information about the noun. For example, "the old wooden table" is a noun phrase where "the old wooden" modifies "table."

A verb phrase consists of a main verb and its auxiliaries or modifiers. For example, "has been reading" is a verb phrase where "has been" supports the main verb "reading." An adjective phrase modifies a noun or pronoun, adding descriptive detail. For instance, "full of energy" in "a child full of energy" describes the child. An adverbial phrase modifies a verb, adjective, or adverb, indicating how, when, where, or why. For example, "with great enthusiasm" in "She spoke with great enthusiasm" explains how she spoke. Both clauses and phrases are integral to sentence construction, providing depth and detail. Clauses form the backbone of sentences, offering complete thoughts or additional information through their various types. Phrases, while lacking a complete subject-predicate structure, enhance sentences by adding specific details and context. Mastery of both elements is essential for crafting clear, engaging, and grammatically accurate communication.

10.1 Independent and Dependent Clauses

In the 9th chapter of "The Fundamentals of English Grammar for Grades 5-10," focusing on clauses and phrases, it is essential to understand the distinction between independent and dependent clauses. These concepts form the backbone of sentence structure, helping to create complex and nuanced expressions in English. Here's a detailed examination of both types of clauses:

1. Independent Clauses

Definition: An independent clause, also known as a main clause, is a group of words that contains a subject and a predicate and expresses a complete thought. It can stand alone as a complete sentence because it doesn't rely on any other clause to make sense.

Characteristics:

- Complete Thought: It expresses a full idea or statement that does not require additional information to be understood.

- Subject and Predicate: It includes both a subject (the doer of the action) and a predicate (the action or state of being).

- Can Stand Alone: It functions independently and doesn't need to be connected to other clauses to form a complete sentence.

2. Dependent Clauses

Definition: A dependent clause, also known as a subordinate clause, is a group of words that contains a subject and a predicate but does not express a complete thought on its own. It relies on an independent clause to give it meaning and context.

Characteristics:

- Incomplete Thought: It does not convey a complete idea by

itself and needs to be attached to an independent clause to make sense.

- Subject and Predicate: It still has a subject and predicate, but these alone do not make it a complete sentence.

- Subordinate Nature: It functions as a subordinate element within a sentence, providing additional information or context.

10.2 Types of Dependent Clauses:

1. **Adjective Clauses**: Modify nouns or pronouns in the main clause. Example: "The book that she borrowed was fascinating." "that she borrowed" is an adjective clause modifying "the book."

2. **Adverbial Clauses**: Modify verbs, adjectives, or adverbs in the main clause and answer questions like why, when, where, or how.Example: "I will call you when I arrive.""when I arrive" is an adverbial clause explaining the timing of the action.

3. **Noun Clauses**: Function as a noun within the main clause, often serving as a subject, object, or complement. Example: "What she said was surprising.""What she said" is a noun clause acting as the subject of the sentence.

10.3 Combining Independent and Dependent Clauses

- **Complex Sentences:**

1. A complex sentence contains one independent clause and at least one dependent clause.

2. Example: "Because she was tired, she went to bed early."

3. "Because she was tired" is a dependent clause providing the reason for the action in the independent clause "she went to bed early."

- **Punctuation:**

1. When the dependent clause comes before the independent

clause: Use a comma to separate them.

2. Example: "If you study hard, you will pass the exam."

3. When the independent clause comes before the dependent clause: No comma is needed.

4. Example: "You will pass the exam if you study hard."

10.4 Understanding the Role in Sentences

- **Creating Complex Sentences**: Using both independent and dependent clauses allows for more detailed and nuanced communication. Complex sentences provide additional context and detail, enriching the content of the message.

- **Enhancing Clarity**: Properly combining and punctuating clauses helps to avoid run-on sentences and fragments, ensuring clarity and coherence in writing.

- **Expanding Ideas**: Dependent clauses allow writers and speakers to expand on their ideas, explain reasons, describe conditions, or add extra information, which can make writing more engaging and informative.

Conclusion

Understanding independent and dependent clauses is crucial for mastering sentence structure and enhancing communication skills. Independent clauses can stand alone as complete sentences, while dependent clauses add depth and detail when combined with independent clauses. By mastering the use of these clauses, you can create more complex, nuanced, and effective sentences, improving both written and spoken communication.

10.1 Types of Phrases (Noun, Verb, Prepositional, etc.)

In grammar, phrases are groups of words that work together to convey a particular meaning within a sentence. Each type of phrase plays a distinct role and contributes to the overall structure and meaning of a sentence. Understanding the different types of phrases—such as noun phrases, verb phrases, adjective phrases, adverb phrases, and prepositional phrases—helps in constructing clear and effective sentences. Here's a detailed look at each type of phrase:

1. Noun Phrase

Definition: A noun phrase consists of a noun (or pronoun) and its modifiers. It functions as a single unit within a sentence and can act as a subject, object, or complement. Structure: Head Noun: The main noun in the phrase. Modifiers: Words or groups of words that describe or limit the noun.

Examples:

- Simple Noun Phrase: "The dog" (where "dog" is the head noun and "the" is the modifier).

- Complex Noun Phrase: "The large brown dog with a red collar" (where "dog" is the head noun, and "the large brown" and "with a red collar" are modifiers).

2. Verb Phrase

Definition: A verb phrase consists of the main verb and its auxiliaries (helping verbs). It conveys the action or state of being in a sentence. Structure: Main Verb: The principal verb that shows the action or state. Auxiliary Verbs: Helping verbs such as "is," "are," "was," "will," "have," "had," etc.

Examples:

- Simple Verb Phrase: "She sings" (where "sings" is the main verb).

- Complex Verb Phrase: "She has been singing beautifully"

(where "has been singing" is the verb phrase, with "has" and "been" as auxiliaries).

3. Adjective Phrase

Definition: An adjective phrase includes an adjective and its modifiers or complements. It describes or qualifies a noun or pronoun in the sentence. Structure: Head Adjective: The main adjective. Modifiers/Complements: Words or phrases that enhance the adjective's meaning.

Examples:

- Simple Adjective Phrase: "Very happy" (where "happy" is the head adjective and "very" is the modifier).

- Complex Adjective Phrase: "Full of excitement and anticipation" (where "full" is the head adjective and "of excitement and anticipation" is the complement).

4. Adverb Phrase

Definition: An adverb phrase consists of an adverb and its modifiers. It modifies verbs, adjectives, or other adverbs, indicating how, when, where, or to what extent something occurs. Structure: Head Adverb: The main adverb. Modifiers: Words or phrases that provide additional detail.

Examples:

- Simple Adverb Phrase: "Quite easily" (where "easily" is the head adverb and "quite" is the modifier).

- Complex Adverb Phrase: "In the early morning light" (where "in the early morning" modifies "light" and provides context).

5. Prepositional Phrase

Definition: A prepositional phrase starts with a preposition and ends with the object of the preposition. It often includes modifiers of the object and provides additional information about time, location, direction, or manner Structure: Preposition: The word that introduces the phrase. Object of the Preposition: The noun or pronoun that follows the preposition. Modifiers: Additional words that modify the object.

Examples:

- Simple Prepositional Phrase: "On the table" (where "on" is the preposition and "the table" is the object).

- Complex Prepositional Phrase: "Under the old oak tree in the park" (where "under" is the preposition, "the

CHAPTER - 11

MODIFIERS

11 Introduction of Modifies

Modifiers are words, phrases, or clauses that provide additional detail and context to other elements in a sentence, enhancing meaning and clarity. Their primary function is to describe, limit, or qualify nouns, pronouns, verbs, adjectives, or adverbs, allowing for more precise and nuanced communication. Modifiers can be categorized into two main types: adjectives and adverbs. Adjectives modify nouns and pronouns by providing more information about them. For instance, in the sentence "The tall building stands in the center of the city," the adjective "tall" modifies the noun "building," specifying its height. Adjectives can describe qualities, quantities, or states, contributing to a richer and more vivid description. Similarly, in "She wore a beautiful dress," "beautiful" modifies "dress," giving insight into the dress's appearance.

Adverbs, on the other hand, modify verbs, adjectives, or other adverbs, offering details about the manner, time, frequency, degree, or place of the action or quality described. For example, in the sentence "He ran quickly to the store," the adverb "quickly" modifies the verb "ran," indicating the speed of the action. Adverbs can also enhance adjectives and other adverbs, as in "She is extremely talented," where "extremely" intensifies the adjective "talented." Modifiers can also appear as phrases and clauses. Adjective phrases consist of an adjective and its related words and modify nouns or pronouns. For example, "the book on the shelf" features the adjective phrase "on the shelf," which describes the noun "book."

Similarly, adverbial phrases modify verbs, adjectives, or adverbs, providing details about how, when, where, or why something occurs. For instance, "with great enthusiasm" in "She spoke with great enthusiasm" describes the manner of her speaking. Adjective clauses and adverbial clauses function similarly to adjective and adverbial phrases but are more complex. An adjective clause modifies a noun or pronoun, adding specific information. For example, "The car that he bought is very expensive," where "that he bought" is the adjective clause describing "car." An adverbial clause modifies verbs, adjectives, or adverbs by providing context such as time, reason, condition, or contrast. For instance, "She stayed home because she was feeling sick," where "because she was feeling sick" is the adverbial clause explaining why she stayed home. Modifiers should be placed close to the word they modify to avoid confusion and ensure clarity.

Misplaced or dangling modifiers can lead to ambiguity or unintended meanings. For example, in the sentence "Walking to the store, the rain started pouring," the modifier "Walking to the store" is mistakenly attached to "the rain," creating confusion. The sentence should be revised to clarify that it was "I" who was walking, such as "Walking to the store, I noticed that the rain started pouring."

a. Adjectives and Adverbs

Adjectives and adverbs are crucial components of sentence structure that enhance the precision and expressiveness of language. Both are used to modify other words, but they serve different functions and apply to different parts of speech. Here's a comprehensive exploration of adjectives and adverbs:

11.1.Adjectives

Definition: Adjectives are words that describe or modify nouns and pronouns. They provide additional information about a noun or pronoun, helping to specify, qualify, or limit its meaning.

- **Functions:**

1. **Descriptive**: Adjectives give details about the size, color, shape, age, or quality of a noun or pronoun. Example: "The blue sky." (The adjective "blue" describes the noun "sky.")

2. **Quantitative**: Adjectives indicate the quantity or amount of a noun. Example: "There are three books on the shelf." (The adjective "three" specifies the number of books.)

3. **Demonstrative**: Adjectives point out specific nouns. Example: "This book is mine." (The adjective "this" specifies which book.)

4. **Possessive**: Adjectives show ownership or relationship. Example: "She wore her new dress." (The adjective "her" indicates ownership of the dress.)

5. **Comparative and Superlative**: Adjectives can express comparisons between two or more things. Comparative: "He is taller than his brother." (The adjective "taller" compares two people.) Superlative: "She is the tallest in the class." (The adjective "tallest" denotes the extreme in a group.)

- **Position in Sentence:**

1. Attributive Position: Adjectives are placed directly before the noun they modify. Example: "A bright idea."

2. Predicative Position: Adjectives follow a linking verb and modify the subject of the sentence. Example: "The idea is bright."

11.1.2 Adverbs

Definition: Adverbs are words that modify verbs, adjectives, or other adverbs. They provide information about how, when, where, or to what extent something happens.

- **Functions:**

1. **Manner**: Adverbs describe how an action is performed. Example: "She sings beautifully." (The adverb "beautifully" describes how she sings.)

2. **Time**: Adverbs indicate when an action occurs. Example: "We will meet tomorrow." (The adverb "tomorrow" tells us when the meeting will take place.)

3. **Place**: Adverbs describe the location of an action. Example: "The children are playing outside." (The adverb "outside" tells us where the children are playing.)

4. **Frequency**: Adverbs indicate how often an action happens. Example: "He rarely eats out." (The adverb "rarely" describes how often he eats out.)

5. **Degree**: Adverbs modify the intensity or degree of an adjective or another adverb. Example: "She is very happy." (The adverb "very" intensifies the adjective "happy.")

- **Position in Sentence:**

1. Before Adjectives: Adverbs modifying adjectives are placed before the adjective.

2. Example: "The movie was incredibly interesting."

3. Before Adverbs: Adverbs modifying other adverbs are placed before the adverb.

4. Example: "She ran quite quickly."

5. At the Beginning or End of a Sentence: Adverbs modifying verbs can be placed at the beginning, end, or middle of a sentence.

6. Example: "Sometimes, I go for a walk." / "I go for a walk

sometimes."

11.2 Placement and Misplacement of Modifiers

Modifiers are words, phrases, or clauses that provide additional information about other elements in a sentence. They can describe, limit, or qualify nouns, pronouns, verbs, adjectives, or adverbs. Correct placement of modifiers ensures clarity and precision in writing, while misplacement can lead to confusion or unintended meanings. Here's an in-depth exploration of the placement and misplacement of modifiers:

11.2.1 Correct Placement of Modifiers

1. Adjective Placement

Adjectives typically precede the nouns they modify when used in the attributive position. When used predicatively, they follow linking verbs.

- Attributive Adjective: "The green apples are delicious."
- The adjective "green" directly modifies the noun "apples."
- Predicative Adjective: "The apples are delicious."
- The adjective "delicious" follows the linking verb "are" and describes the noun "apples."

2. Adverb Placement

Adverbs can be placed in various positions depending on what they modify:

- Before Adjectives or Adverbs: "She is very talented."
- The adverb "very" modifies the adjective "talented."
- Before Verbs: "He runs quickly."
- The adverb "quickly" modifies the verb "runs."
- At the Beginning or End of Sentences: "Usually, I go for a jog in the morning."

- The adverb "usually" modifies the entire sentence, indicating frequency.

3. Prepositional Phrases

Prepositional phrases provide additional detail about nouns or verbs and should be placed as close as possible to the words they modify to avoid ambiguity.

- Modifying Nouns: "The book on the shelf is new."
- The prepositional phrase "on the shelf" modifies the noun "book."
- Modifying Verbs: "She spoke to the audience with confidence."
- The prepositional phrase "with confidence" modifies the verb "spoke."

4. Participial Phrases

Participial phrases should be placed next to the noun or pronoun they modify to clearly indicate what is being described.

- Example: "Walking through the park, she found a lost dog."
- The participial phrase "Walking through the park" modifies "she," indicating the action she was doing when she found the dog.

11.2.2 Misplacement of Modifiers

1. Dangling Modifiers

A dangling modifier is a word or phrase that is not clearly or logically related to the word it is intended to modify, often leading to confusion. Example: "Walking to the store, the rain started pouring." Here, "Walking to the store" seems to modify "the rain," which is illogical. The correct sentence should specify the person walking: "Walking to the store, she noticed that the rain started pouring."

2. Misplaced Modifiers

A misplaced modifier is positioned in a sentence such that it creates ambiguity or suggests an unintended meaning. Example: "She almost drove her kids to school every day." The placement of "almost" suggests that she did not drive them every day but nearly did. The intended meaning might be: "She drove her kids to school almost every day."

3. Squinting Modifiers

A squinting modifier is placed ambiguously between two words or phrases, making it unclear which it is intended to modify. Example: "Running quickly improves your health." It is unclear whether "quickly" modifies "running" or "improves." The intended meaning can be clarified by rephrasing: "If you run quickly, you will improve your health."

11.2.3 Examples of Misplaced Modifiers

1. **Misplaced Modifier**: "I saw a man on a bike who was very friendly." This sentence implies that the man on the bike was very friendly. The intended meaning might be: "I saw a very friendly man on a bike."

2. **Dangling Modifier**: "After reading the book, the movie was disappointing." The sentence implies that "the movie" was reading the book, which is incorrect. The sentence should be: "After reading the book, I found the movie disappointing."

3. **Squinting Modifier**: "He almost drove to the office every day." The word "almost" creates ambiguity about whether he drove every day or nearly every day. The sentence can be clarified: "He drove to the office almost every day."

11.2.4 How to Avoid Misplaced Modifiers

1. Place Modifiers Near the Words They Modify: Ensure that modifiers are positioned close to the words they are intended to

modify to avoid ambiguity.

- Correct: "She wore a dress with a floral pattern to the party."
- Incorrect: "She wore a dress to the party with a floral pattern."

2. Be Clear About What the Modifier is Describing: Make sure the modifier clearly and logically describes the intended word or phrase.

- Correct: "He found a wallet lost in the park."
- Incorrect: "He found a lost wallet in the park."

3. Check for Dangling Modifiers: Ensure that modifiers have a clear, logical subject in the sentence.

- Correct: "While walking through the park, she found a wallet."
- Incorrect: "While walking through the park, a wallet was found."

Conclusion

Correct placement of modifiers is crucial for clear and precise communication. Modifiers enhance sentences by adding detail and nuance but must be positioned carefully to avoid misplacement and ambiguity. By understanding the roles and proper placement of adjectives, adverbs, and other modifiers, you can improve the clarity and effectiveness of your writing.

CHAPTER - 12

COMPLEX SENTENCE STRUCTURES

- **Introduction of Complex Sentence Structures**

Complex sentences are integral to sophisticated writing, allowing for the integration of multiple ideas into a single, nuanced statement. They consist of one independent clause and at least one dependent clause, creating a structure that conveys detailed and interconnected information. The independent clause, or main clause, stands alone as a complete thought with a subject and predicate, while the dependent clause, or subordinate clause, cannot stand alone and provides additional context or detail to the main clause. Complex sentences enhance writing by enabling the expression of more intricate ideas and relationships between different parts of a sentence. Dependent clauses, which can function as adjective, adverbial, or noun clauses, add specificity and depth. Adjective clauses modify nouns or pronouns, offering extra details, such as in "The book that she borrowed was fascinating," where "that she borrowed" specifies the book.

Adverbial clauses modify verbs, adjectives, or other adverbs, providing context like time, reason, or manner, as seen in "I will call you when I arrive," where "when I arrive" indicates the timing of the call. Noun clauses, on the other hand, act as subjects, objects, or complements, exemplified by "What she said was surprising," where "What she said" serves as the subject of the sentence. The placement of dependent clauses can vary. When they precede the independent clause, they are usually followed by a comma, such as in "If it stops raining, we can go for a walk." When they follow the independent clause, commas are generally not needed unless the clause adds non-essential information, as in "We can go for a walk if it stops raining." Misplacement or dangling of these clauses can lead to confusion or ambiguity, underscoring the importance of correct positioning to maintain clarity. Complex sentences are powerful tools in writing, offering the ability to express detailed and layered ideas. They contribute to richer, more engaging communication by linking related thoughts and providing a deeper understanding of the subject matter. Mastery of complex sentence structures enables writers to convey a wide range of information with precision and nuance, enhancing both written and spoken discourse.

12.1 Compound-Complex Sentences

A compound-complex sentence blends the structures of compound and complex sentences, combining at least two independent clauses with one or more dependent clauses.

This structure allows for the conveyance of intricate ideas by integrating multiple main thoughts with additional contextual or conditional details. Independent Clauses in a compound-complex sentence are complete thoughts that can stand alone as sentences. For instance, in the sentence "She wanted to go to the park, and he agreed to join her," both "She wanted to go to the park" and "he agreed to join her" are independent clauses. They are connected by the coordinating conjunction "and," illustrating a compound sentence structure. Adding a dependent clause to such a combination, as in "Although it was raining, she wanted to go to the park, and he agreed to join her," introduces additional context. Here,

"Although it was raining" is a dependent clause that sets a condition affecting the main actions.Dependent Clauses cannot stand alone and rely on the independent clauses for complete meaning. They often add detail, context, or conditions. For example, in "We will go to the beach if the weather improves, and we will bring a picnic if we find a good spot," the adverbial clauses "if the weather improves" and "if we find a good spot" set conditions for the actions described in the independent clauses.

This arrangement allows for a more detailed and nuanced expression of the conditions affecting the main actions.Proper punctuation in compound-complex sentences is essential for clarity. When independent clauses are connected by a coordinating conjunction (for, and, nor, but, or, yet, so), a comma is used before the conjunction. For instance, "She wanted to go to the park, but it was raining, so they stayed home" uses commas to separate the independent clauses. When a dependent clause precedes the independent clauses, it is generally followed by a comma, as in "Although it was raining, she wanted to go to the park, and he agreed to join her." This punctuation helps to clarify the relationship between the clauses and avoid ambiguity. Compound-complex sentences enhance writing by allowing the expression of detailed and nuanced ideas, linking multiple independent clauses with context provided by dependent clauses. This structure not only adds depth to writing but also helps to clearly articulate complex relationships and conditions. Mastery of compound-complex sentences contributes to more sophisticated, engaging, and precise communication.

12.2 Subordination and Coordination

Subordination and coordination are fundamental concepts in sentence structure that help organize and articulate complex ideas within a sentence. These techniques allow for the combination of clauses in ways that clarify relationships and enhance the depth of expression.

Subordination involves connecting a dependent clause to an independent clause, allowing one part of the sentence to provide additional information or context about the main idea. A dependent clause cannot stand alone as a complete sentence because it does not express a complete thought. Instead, it relies on an independent clause to give it meaning. By using subordination, writers can include subordinate details that explain, qualify, or expand on the main idea. For instance, in the sentence "Although she was tired, she finished her homework," the dependent clause "Although she was tired" introduces a condition that affects the independent clause "she finished her homework." This use of subordination provides a nuanced view of the circumstances surrounding the action in the main clause, offering a more detailed picture of the situation.Subordinate clauses often function as adverbial, adjective, or noun clauses.

Adverbial clauses modify verbs, adjectives, or adverbs by providing context such as time, cause, or condition. For example, "If it rains tomorrow, we will cancel the picnic" uses the adverbial clause "If it rains tomorrow" to set a condition for the action in the main clause. Adjective clauses describe or limit nouns, as seen in "The book that she borrowed was fascinating," where "that she borrowed" provides additional information about "the book." Noun clauses act as subjects, objects, or complements, such as in "What you said was true," where "What you said" serves as the subject of the sentence. Coordination, on the other hand, connects two or more independent clauses of equal importance using coordinating conjunctions like "and," "but," "or," "nor," "for," "so," and "yet." These conjunctions join clauses that can each stand alone as complete sentences, thereby linking ideas of equal weight within a single sentence.

For example, "She wanted to go for a walk, but it was too cold" combines two independent clauses—"She wanted to go for a walk" and "it was too cold"—with the conjunction "but," showing a contrast between the two ideas. Coordination allows each clause to retain its own significance while contributing to the overall meaning of the sentence, thus creating a clear and balanced expression of related ideas. Both subordination and coordination are crucial for crafting well-structured and effective sentences. Subordination adds depth and complexity by allowing writers to embed additional information and context within their sentences. It helps to convey relationships between different pieces of information and enriches the narrative with detailed explanations. Coordination, by linking independent clauses, provides a means to present multiple ideas in a cohesive manner, emphasizing their equal importance and creating a rhythm in writing. Mastering these techniques enables writers to produce sentences that are both clear and sophisticated. Subordination helps articulate complex relationships and conditions, while coordination ensures that related ideas are presented with equal weight. Together, they enhance the ability to communicate nuanced and detailed thoughts effectively.

CHAPTER - 13

AGREEMENT

13 Introduction of Agreement

Agreement in grammar refers to the consistency between different elements of a sentence, primarily concerning the alignment of subjects and verbs, as well as nouns and their modifiers, to ensure clarity and correctness in writing. The principle of agreement is crucial for maintaining coherence and comprehensibility in both simple and complex sentences. Subject-Verb Agreement is one of the most fundamental aspects of agreement. It requires that the verb in a sentence match the subject in both number (singular or plural) and person. For example, in the sentence "She writes daily," the singular subject "She" is matched with the singular verb "writes." Conversely, in "They write daily," the plural subject "They" is paired with the plural verb "write."

This consistency ensures that the verb accurately reflects the subject's number and person, making the sentence clear and grammatically correct. Noun-Pronoun Agreement is another important aspect of agreement. Pronouns must agree with the nouns they replace in gender, number, and person. For instance, in "The teacher gave her students their assignments," the pronouns "her" and "their" agree with the singular noun "teacher" and the plural noun "students," respectively. This agreement prevents ambiguity and maintains the clarity of which nouns the pronouns refer to. Modifiers must also agree with the nouns they modify in terms of number and sometimes gender. For example, "The tall man" and

"The tall men" demonstrate how adjectives and nouns must match in number to convey precise meaning. Incorrect agreement, such as "The tall men is here," disrupts the sentence's clarity and correctness.

In complex sentences, agreement extends to the consistency between clauses. For example, in the sentence "The book that was on the table has been moved," the verb "was" in the dependent clause "that was on the table" agrees with the singular subject "book," while the verb "has been moved" in the independent clause agrees with "book" as well. This ensures that each part of the sentence maintains logical and grammatical consistency. Overall, maintaining agreement in writing is essential for producing clear and grammatically accurate sentences. It ensures that all elements of the sentence work together cohesively, avoiding confusion and enhancing the readability and professionalism of the text.

By adhering to the rules of agreement, writers can effectively communicate their ideas and maintain the structural integrity of their sentences.

13.1 Subject-Verb Agreement

Subject-Verb Agreement is a fundamental rule in grammar that requires the verb in a sentence to correspond in number and person with the subject. This principle ensures that sentences are clear and grammatically correct, facilitating effective communication.

13.1 .1 Basic Rules of Subject-Verb Agreement

1. Singular and Plural Subjects:

- Singular Subjects: When the subject is singular, the verb must also be singular. For example, "The cat runs quickly." Here, "cat" is a singular subject, and "runs" is the singular form of the verb.

- Plural Subjects: When the subject is plural, the verb must be plural. For instance, "The cats run quickly." In this case, "cats" is a plural subject, and "run" is the plural form of the verb.

2. **Subjects Joined by "And":**

- When two or more singular subjects are joined by "and," they form a plural subject, requiring a plural verb. For example, "The teacher and the student are in the classroom." Both "teacher" and "student" are singular, but together they form a plural subject, so the verb "are" is used.

3. **Subjects Joined by "Or" or "Nor":**

- When subjects are joined by "or" or "nor," the verb should agree with the subject closest to it. For example, "Either the manager or the employees are responsible for the error." Here, "employees" is plural, so the verb "are" agrees with it.

4. **Indefinite Pronouns:**

- Indefinite pronouns like "everyone," "someone," "each," and "nobody" are considered singular and require singular verbs. For example, "Everyone is excited about the event."

- Conversely, pronouns such as "several," "few," "both," and "many" are plural and require plural verbs. For instance, "Many were surprised by the results."

5. **Collective Nouns:**

- Collective nouns, which refer to groups composed of individuals, can be singular or plural based on whether the group acts as a single unit or individually.

For instance, "The team is winning" (singular) versus "The team are arguing among themselves" (plural).

6. Titles and Names:

- Titles of books, movies, and other works, as well as names of organizations, are treated as singular even if they refer to multiple people or entities. For example, "The United Nations is headquartered in New York."

13.1.2 Complex Sentences and Agreement

In complex sentences, maintaining subject-verb agreement requires attention to both the main clause and any subordinate clauses. The verb in the main clause must agree with the subject of that clause. For instance, "The book that the teacher recommended is on the shelf." Here, "The book" is the subject of the main clause, and "is" is the verb that agrees with it. The dependent clause "that the teacher recommended" does not affect the agreement in the main clause.

13.1.3 Common Pitfalls and Exceptions

- Compound Subjects: When subjects are connected by "and," they typically form a plural subject, but exceptions exist. For example, "Macaroni and cheese is my favorite dish." In this case, the subject is considered singular because it refers to a single dish.

- Amount Expressions: Expressions of amount or quantity such as "a group of," "a number of," or "a lot of" can affect verb agreement. For example, "A number of students are participating," where "students" is plural, and "is" in "A group of students is" where "group" is singular.

Subject-Verb Agreement is essential for clear, precise communication. Adhering to these rules helps maintain grammatical accuracy and ensures that sentences convey the intended meaning without confusion.

13.2 Pronoun-Antecedent Agreement

Pronoun-Antecedent Agreement is a crucial aspect of grammatical correctness that ensures pronouns and their antecedents (the nouns they replace) agree in number, gender, and person. This agreement is essential for clarity and coherence in writing, helping readers easily understand which nouns are being referred to.

13.2.1 Basic Rules of Pronoun-Antecedent Agreement

1. Number Agreement:

- Singular Antecedents: A singular noun must be matched with a singular pronoun. For example, "The teacher lost his keys." Here, "teacher" is singular, and the pronoun "his" correctly refers back to it.

- Plural Antecedents: A plural noun requires a plural pronoun. For instance, "The students completed their assignments on time." The plural noun "students" is correctly matched with the plural pronoun "their."

2. Gender Agreement:

- Pronouns must match the gender of their antecedents. For example, "The woman gave her presentation." The pronoun "her" correctly refers to "woman," which is feminine.

- For gender-neutral situations, the use of singular "they" has become widely accepted to avoid specifying gender. For example, "Each student should bring their own lunch," where "their" refers to "each student" without indicating gender.

3. Person Agreement:

- Pronouns must align in person with their antecedents. If the antecedent is in the first person, the pronoun should also be in the first person. For instance, "I will handle my responsibilities." Here,

"I" (first person) and "my" (first person) agree.

- Similarly, for third-person antecedents, the pronouns should be in the third person. For example, "He said that he would call me later." Both "He" and "he" are third-person pronouns that match the antecedent "He."

13.2.2 Complex Cases and Exceptions

1. Compound Antecedents: When the antecedent is a compound subject (joined by "and"), it is typically treated as plural, requiring a plural pronoun. For example, "Tom and Jerry said they would join us." The compound subject "Tom and Jerry" is plural, so the pronoun "they" is used. However, when the compound antecedent is joined by "or" or "nor," the pronoun must agree with the closest antecedent. For example, "Either the manager or the employees will present their report." Since "employees" is plural, the pronoun "their" is used.

2. Collective Nouns: Collective nouns such as "team," "group," or "family" may be singular or plural depending on whether the group is acting as a single unit or as individuals. For instance, "The team has completed its project" (acting as a single unit) versus "The team are taking their seats" (acting as individuals).

3. Indefinite Pronouns: Indefinite pronouns like "everyone," "somebody," "none," and "each" are typically treated as singular and require singular pronouns. For example, "Everyone should bring his or her own lunch." However, plural indefinite pronouns such as "both," "few," "several," and "many" require plural pronouns. For example, "Many brought their own books."

13.3 Importance of Pronoun-Antecedent Agreement

Proper pronoun-antecedent agreement is essential for clear and effective communication. It prevents confusion by ensuring that pronouns unambiguously refer to their antecedents, thus enhancing the reader's understanding of the text. Agreement helps maintain grammatical accuracy and coherence, making the writing more professional and readable In summary, adhering to pronoun-antecedent agreement rules ensures that pronouns and their antecedents consistently match in number, gender, and person. This practice is vital for producing clear, coherent, and grammatically correct writing.

CHAPTER - 14

ADVANCED PUNCTUATION

14 Introduction of Punctuations

Advanced punctuation plays a crucial role in enhancing the clarity, meaning, and flow of complex writing. Beyond basic punctuation marks like periods, commas, and question marks, advanced punctuation includes the use of colons, semicolons, dashes, and parentheses, which help manage intricate sentence structures and convey nuanced meaning. Colons are used to introduce lists, explanations, or elaborations. They signal that what follows will provide more detail or complete the thought started before the colon. For example, "She had three goals: to improve her skills, to gain experience, and to earn a promotion." Here, the colon introduces a list of goals, providing specifics that elaborate on the initial statement. Colons are also used before a quotation when the preceding clause is a complete sentence.

For instance, "He made an important point: 'Success is not final, failure is not fatal.'" This usage emphasizes the significance of the quote. Semicolons function as a bridge between closely related independent clauses that are not joined by a conjunction. They provide a way to link ideas that are related but could stand alone as separate sentences. For instance, "The project was completed on time; however, it did not meet all the requirements." The semicolon here connects two independent clauses, while "however" introduces a contrast. Semicolons are also used in complex lists where items themselves contain commas, providing clarity and avoiding confusion.

For example, "The conference will be attended by John Smith, the project manager; Mary Jones, the chief engineer; and Emily Davis, the HR director." This usage helps to delineate the items in the list clearly. Dashes are versatile punctuation marks used to create emphasis, show interruptions, or indicate additional information. An em dash (—) can be used to set off parenthetical elements or abrupt changes in thought, as in "The results of the experiment—though preliminary—are promising." The em dash provides a pause that draws attention to the inserted information. In dialogue or narrative writing, dashes can indicate interruptions or abrupt shifts in speech, such as "I was just thinking—oh, never mind." Additionally, dashes can replace commas or parentheses for stylistic reasons, offering a more informal or emphatic tone. Parentheses enclose supplementary information or clarifications that are not essential to the main point but provide additional context.

For example, "The committee will meet next week (on Tuesday, if the schedule permits) to finalize the plans." The information in parentheses adds details without disrupting the flow of the main sentence. Parentheses are useful for including references, asides, or explanations that enhance understanding without altering the core message. Ellipses (...) indicate omitted material or a pause in speech. They can show where text has been removed from a quotation or where there is an intentional pause in dialogue or thought. For example, "The report was due on Friday, but..." suggests an incomplete thought or a trailing off of speech. In quotations, ellipses are used to indicate that part of the text has been omitted, such as "She said, 'I'm not sure... I'll have to check.'" Advanced punctuation marks like colons, semicolons, dashes, parentheses, and ellipses enrich writing by allowing for more sophisticated expression and clearer communication of complex ideas. They help to organize information, manage the flow of thoughts, and provide emphasis where needed. Mastery of these punctuation marks enables writers to craft precise and nuanced sentences that effectively convey their intended meaning and enhance the readability of their work.

14.1 Usage of Dashes, Parentheses, Ellipses

Dashes, parentheses, and ellipses are essential punctuation marks that add depth and clarity to writing, each serving distinct purposes to refine and articulate complex ideas. Dashes, particularly the em dash (—) and the en dash (–), are versatile tools in punctuation. The em dash is frequently used to create emphasis or insert additional information within a sentence. It can replace commas, parentheses, or colons, offering a way to highlight or set off parenthetical information with greater impact. For example, in the sentence "The concert—though initially sold out—was later rescheduled," the em dashes frame the interjected detail about the concert's rescheduling, drawing attention to it without breaking the sentence's flow.

This usage can also reflect abrupt changes in thought or interruptions, particularly in dialogue. Consider "I was thinking about going to the beach—oh, wait, it's supposed to rain." Here, the em dash signals a sudden shift in the speaker's thought, adding a conversational tone. The en dash, on the other hand, is shorter than the em dash and is used primarily to indicate ranges or connections between related items. It's commonly seen in contexts such as dates, times, or numerical ranges. For example, "The exhibition runs from April 1–June 30" uses the en dash to connect the start and end dates of the event, clearly showing the duration. It also links related terms, such as in "The New York–London flight," where it signifies the relationship between the two cities.

This usage helps in maintaining clarity and avoiding confusion in complex lists or ranges. Parentheses serve a different function by enclosing supplementary or clarifying information that adds context but is not crucial to the main point of the sentence. They help provide additional details or asides without disrupting the primary narrative. For instance, "The new policy will take effect next month (August, to be precise) and will impact all departments." The parentheses offer extra detail about the specific month, enhancing the reader's understanding without overshadowing the main message. Parentheses can also be used to insert tangential comments or explanations. For example, "Her novel, a bestseller in several countries (including the UK and Australia), has received critical acclaim." Here, the information within parentheses provides interesting but non-essential detail about the novel's success in different regions. This helps in keeping the main text focused while still delivering additional context. Ellipses (...) are used to indicate omitted material, pauses, or unfinished thoughts. They are particularly useful in quotations to show that part of the original text has been removed for brevity or relevance.

For example, "The report stated, 'The results were inconclusive... more studies are necessary.'" The ellipses suggest that some content has been omitted, focusing on the essential part of the statement. Ellipses can also convey hesitation or create a conversational tone by indicating pauses or incomplete thoughts. For instance, "I was thinking... maybe we should reconsider our strategy," uses ellipses to show a pause or uncertainty in the speaker's thought. This usage adds a reflective or tentative quality to the sentence. Additionally, ellipses can signal that a statement is trailing off or incomplete, which can create a sense of suspense or leave something open-ended. For example, "I never imagined he would..." implies that there's more to the thought that remains unsaid, inviting the reader to fill in the gaps. In summary, dashes, parentheses, and ellipses are advanced punctuation marks that enhance writing by providing ways to manage complex sentence structures, emphasize specific details, and convey nuanced meanings. The em dash offers flexibility in setting off information and managing interruptions, the en dash connects related items and ranges, parentheses enclose additional context or asides, and ellipses indicate omissions, pauses, or unfinished thoughts. Mastering these punctuation marks allows writers to craft sentences that are not only grammatically correct but also rich in clarity and expressiveness.

14.2 Hyphenation Rule

Hyphenation rules are crucial for ensuring clarity and precision in writing, helping to prevent confusion and maintain readability. Hyphens are used to connect words and parts of words, and understanding their correct usage is essential for effective communication. Hyphens are primarily employed in three key areas: compound adjectives, compound nouns, and word divisions at the end of lines. Their use can vary based on specific rules and conventions, which are essential to grasp for clear and professional writing. Compound Adjectives: When two or more words work together to modify a noun, they form a compound adjective. Hyphens are used to link these words to avoid ambiguity and clarify that they function as a single descriptor. For example, "a well-known author" uses hyphens to show that "well" and "known" together describe "author."

Without the hyphens, the phrase could be misinterpreted as "a known author who is well," altering the intended meaning. Similarly, "a high-quality product" uses hyphens to link "high" and "quality," ensuring that the two words jointly modify "product." Hyphens are essential here because they prevent confusion that might arise if the words were read separately. However, hyphenation rules for compound adjectives can change based on the position in the sentence. When compound adjectives precede the noun they modify, hyphens are typically used. For example, "an up-to-date report" and "a state-of-the-art facility" both use hyphens to clarify that "up-to-date" and "state-of-the-art" are single adjectives describing the nouns "report" and "facility," respectively. When the compound adjective follows the noun, hyphens are usually omitted.

For instance, "The report is up to date" and "The facility is state of the art" do not require hyphens because the adjectives are no longer directly modifying the noun in a compound form. Compound Nouns: Hyphens are also used in compound nouns, where two or more words combine to create a single noun. For instance, "mother-in-law" and "well-being" are hyphenated compounds. The hyphen helps to link the words and indicates that they function together as a single noun. This use of hyphens prevents misreading and ensures that the compound noun is understood as a cohesive unit rather than separate words. In some cases, compound nouns can be written with or without hyphens, depending on established usage or preference. For example, "email" can be written as "e-mail," and both forms are acceptable. The decision to use a hyphen often depends on the evolution of language and stylistic preferences, but consistency is key in any written document. Word Divisions:

Hyphens are also used to divide words at the end of a line when they are too long to fit within the margins. The goal is to break the word in a way that maintains readability and avoids awkward splits. Standard rules for word division include breaking words between syllables and avoiding division after prefixes or before suffixes. For example, "incredible" can be divided as "in-cred-ible" but should not be split as "incred-ible." Proper hyphenation at line breaks ensures that words remain recognizable and readable, improving the overall presentation of the text. Special Cases and Exceptions: Certain words and phrases have specific hyphenation rules. For example, many prefixes and suffixes are not hyphenated, such as "prepaid" or "nonsmoker." Additionally, some compound adjectives that include adverbs ending in "-ly" do not require hyphens, such as "highly effective" or "quickly finished." These exceptions are guided by usage conventions and specific style guides, so it is important to consult relevant resources when in doubt. In summary, hyphenation rules are fundamental for maintaining clarity and precision in writing. They are used in compound adjectives to link descriptive words, in compound nouns to form cohesive units, and in word divisions to ensure readability at line breaks. By understanding and applying these rules, writers can produce text that is not only grammatically correct but also clear and easy to read.

CHAPTER - 15

WRITING STYLE AND CLARITY

15 Introduction of Writing

Writing style and clarity are fundamental elements of effective communication that significantly impact how well a message is received and understood. Developing a clear and engaging writing style involves a combination of careful word choice, sentence structure, and organization, all aimed at enhancing readability and ensuring that the intended message is conveyed accurately. Writing style encompasses the unique voice and tone a writer employs, which reflects their personality, perspective, and purpose. It includes choices about vocabulary, sentence length, and overall tone. A writer's style can range from formal and academic to casual and conversational, depending on the audience and context.

For instance, academic writing often utilizes a formal style with precise terminology and complex sentence structures, while blog writing might be more informal and engaging, using simpler language and shorter sentences. The key is to match the writing style to the audience's expectations and the purpose of the communication. Consistency in style is crucial for maintaining clarity and ensuring that the message is coherent. Inconsistent style can confuse readers and detract from the effectiveness of the writing. For example, switching between formal and informal tones within a single document can disrupt the reader's understanding and engagement. Similarly, a mix of technical jargon and layman's terms without clear explanations can alienate readers who are unfamiliar with the subject matter. Clarity in writing involves presenting ideas in a straightforward and unambiguous manner. Achieving clarity requires careful attention to several elements:

- **Word Choice:** Using precise and appropriate vocabulary is essential for clear communication. Avoiding overly complex or ambiguous words helps ensure that the message is understood as intended. For example, instead of using "utilize," which may sound overly formal, "use" might be clearer and more straightforward. Additionally, selecting the right words for the context can help convey the intended meaning without causing confusion.

- **Sentence Structure:** Simple and well-structured sentences contribute to clarity. Complex sentences with multiple clauses can be difficult to follow and may obscure the main point. Breaking down complex ideas into simpler, shorter sentences can enhance readability.

For instance, instead of writing "Despite the fact that the project was delayed due to unforeseen circumstances, which caused a significant disruption to the schedule, the team managed to complete it on time," one could write, "The project was delayed due to unforeseen circumstances, disrupting the schedule. However, the team still completed it on time." This revision breaks the information into more digestible parts and makes the message clearer.

- **Paragraph Organization**: Well-organized paragraphs help guide the reader through the text and support the overall flow of ideas. Each paragraph should focus on a single main idea and be logically structured to build upon the preceding content. Effective transitions between paragraphs help maintain coherence and guide the reader through the argument or narrative. For example, starting a paragraph with a topic sentence that clearly states the main point, followed by supporting details and examples, creates a clear and logical progression of ideas.

- **Avoiding Ambiguity**: To ensure clarity, it's important to avoid ambiguous language and provide sufficient context for the reader to understand the message. Ambiguities can arise from vague wording, unclear pronoun references, or lack of detail. For instance, instead of writing "The results were impressive," specify what results were being referred to and why they were impressive: "The sales results for Q2 exceeded expectations by 20%, demonstrating the effectiveness of the new marketing strategy."

- **Editing and Proofreading**: Revising and proofreading are critical steps in achieving clarity. Editing allows writers to refine their ideas, correct errors, and improve the overall structure of the text. Proofreading helps catch grammatical mistakes, typos, and inconsistencies that can detract from the clarity of the writing. Rereading the text from the perspective of a reader unfamiliar with the content can help identify areas where further clarification is needed.

In summary, a clear and effective writing style is achieved through thoughtful word choice, well-structured sentences, and coherent paragraph organization. Matching the writing style to the audience and purpose, avoiding ambiguity, and diligently editing and proofreading all contribute to enhanced readability and communication. By focusing on these aspects, writers can ensure that their messages are both engaging and easily understood, making their communication more impactful and effective.

15.2 Avoiding Run-on Sentences

Avoiding run-on sentences is essential for maintaining clarity and readability in writing. Run-on sentences occur when two or more independent clauses are incorrectly joined together without appropriate punctuation or conjunctions. This can lead to confusion and obscure the meaning of the text, making it challenging for readers to follow the writer's intended message. Understanding how to identify and correct run-on sentences is crucial for clear and effective writing. Run-on sentences often result from improper or missing punctuation between independent clauses. An independent clause is a group of words that contains a subject and a predicate and expresses a complete thought. For example, in the run-on sentence "I went to the store I forgot to buy milk," there are two independent clauses—"I went to the store" and "I forgot to buy milk"—that are incorrectly joined without punctuation or a coordinating conjunction.

To correct run-on sentences, one can use several strategies. The first approach is to separate the independent clauses with a period. This method creates two distinct sentences, which can make the text clearer and easier to understand. For instance, the run-on sentence "I went to the store I forgot to buy milk" can be revised to "I went to the store. I forgot to buy milk." By breaking the sentence into two separate sentences, each idea is given its own space, improving clarity. Another effective strategy is to use a comma followed by a coordinating conjunction. Coordinating conjunctions—such as and, but, or, nor, for, so, and yet—connect independent clauses and help clarify the relationship between them. For example, "I went to the store, but I forgot to buy milk" correctly uses a comma and the conjunction "but" to join the two clauses, indicating a contrast between the two ideas.

This approach maintains the flow of the text while ensuring that each independent clause is properly connected. Using a semicolon is another way to address run-on sentences. A semicolon can link closely related independent clauses without using a conjunction. For instance, "I went to the store; I forgot to buy milk" uses a semicolon to join the two clauses, suggesting that the ideas are related but should be distinct. Semicolons are particularly useful for connecting independent clauses that are closely related in meaning but do not require a conjunction. Incorporating subordinate clauses is another technique to avoid run-on sentences. By turning one of the independent clauses into a dependent clause, a writer can combine ideas more seamlessly. For example, "I went to the store because I needed to buy milk" converts the second clause into a dependent clause, creating a single, coherent sentence.

Subordinate clauses provide additional context and can help clarify the relationship between different parts of a sentence. Revising complex sentences to ensure clarity and coherence can also help prevent run-on sentences. Breaking down complex ideas into simpler sentences or using proper punctuation can make the text more readable. For example, "Although I went to the store, I forgot to buy milk" introduces the dependent clause "Although I went to the store" and then provides the main idea "I forgot to buy milk." This structure helps clearly separate the introductory information from the main point. Editing and proofreading are crucial steps in identifying and correcting run-on sentences.

During the revision process, writers should carefully review their sentences to ensure that independent clauses are properly punctuated and connected. Reading the text aloud can help catch run-on sentences, as the natural flow of speech often reveals awkward or confusing sentence structures. Additionally, using grammar-checking tools can assist in identifying potential run-on sentences, though manual review remains essential for ensuring accuracy and clarity. In summary, avoiding run-on sentences involves understanding how to properly connect independent clauses using periods, commas with conjunctions, semicolons, and subordinate clauses. By applying these strategies and focusing on clear, coherent sentence structure, writers can enhance the readability of their text and ensure that their ideas are communicated effectively. Through careful editing and proofreading, writers can identify and correct run-on sentences, improving the overall quality of their writing.

15.3 Avoiding Sentence Fragments

Avoiding sentence fragments is vital for producing clear and coherent writing. Sentence fragments, which are incomplete sentences that lack a main clause, can disrupt the flow of text and confuse readers. These fragments often result from missing subjects or predicates, or they might be dependent clauses that are mistakenly presented as complete sentences. Understanding how to identify and correct sentence fragments is essential for ensuring that writing is both precise and effective. A sentence fragment typically fails to meet the criteria for a complete sentence. A complete sentence must have at least one independent clause, which includes a subject and a predicate and expresses a complete thought. For example, "Although I went to the store" is a fragment because it is a dependent clause that doesn't stand alone as a complete thought. In contrast, "Although I went to the store, I forgot to buy milk" is a complete sentence because it combines the dependent clause with an independent clause, thus providing a complete thought.

To avoid sentence fragments, it is crucial to ensure that each sentence contains a subject and a predicate and expresses a complete idea. One effective approach is to review each sentence and confirm that it includes a main clause. For instance, a fragment such as "Because I was tired" lacks a main clause and needs to be revised. Adding a complete thought, such as "Because I was tired, I went to bed early," creates a full sentence by combining the fragment with an independent clause. Another common type of fragment is the one that occurs when a dependent clause is mistakenly used as a complete sentence. Dependent clauses rely on an independent clause to form a complete thought. For example, "When the meeting was over" is a dependent clause that needs an independent clause to complete the thought. By revising it to "When the meeting was over, we went out for dinner," the dependent clause is properly integrated into a complete sentence, providing the necessary context. Fragments can also result from the misuse of introductory phrases.

For instance, "After the long day" might be an introductory phrase that sets up an expectation for a complete thought. However, if it is left isolated, it becomes a fragment. Correcting this involves completing the thought, such as in "After the long day, I was relieved to finally relax." This revision links the introductory phrase to a main clause, making it a complete sentence. Another frequent cause of sentence fragments is the use of isolated noun phrases or verb phrases without a complete predicate or subject. For example, "A delicious meal" is a noun phrase that lacks a verb, making it a fragment. To correct this, incorporate a verb and create a full sentence: "The chef prepared a delicious meal." This addition of a verb provides the necessary action, completing the thought and forming a proper sentence.

To ensure that sentences are complete, writers should pay attention to common fragment pitfalls, such as missing subjects, incomplete predicates, or disconnected clauses. Reviewing sentences for these issues and revising accordingly can help prevent fragments. One useful technique is to read sentences out loud or use sentence diagramming to visually map out the structure, ensuring that each sentence includes all necessary components. Additionally, editing and proofreading are crucial in identifying and correcting sentence fragments. During the revision process, writers should scrutinize their sentences to ensure that each one is complete and coherent. Tools such as grammar checkers can assist in spotting fragments, though manual review is essential for a thorough examination. Reading the text from a fresh perspective or having another person review it can also help in catching fragments that might be overlooked. In summary, avoiding sentence fragments involves ensuring that each sentence contains a subject, a predicate, and expresses a complete thought.

By carefully reviewing sentences, integrating dependent clauses with independent clauses, and avoiding isolated phrases, writers can maintain the clarity and coherence of their text. Through diligent editing and proofreading, writers can identify and correct fragments, resulting in writing that is both precise and effective.

15.4 Parallel Structure

Parallel structure, also known as parallelism, is a fundamental principle in writing that involves using consistent grammatical forms within sentences or across sentences to create balance and clarity. This technique helps to organize ideas in a way that enhances readability and reinforces the logical flow of the text. By maintaining a parallel structure, writers ensure that their ideas are presented in a clear, cohesive manner, making it easier for readers to follow and understand the content. Parallel structure is achieved by aligning similar grammatical elements, such as words, phrases, or clauses, within a sentence or between sentences. For example, in the sentence "She enjoys reading, writing, and hiking," the parallel structure is evident in the consistent use of gerunds (reading, writing, hiking) to describe her interests. This parallelism creates a rhythm and balance that makes the sentence more engaging and easier to comprehend. One of the key benefits of parallel structure is that it enhances readability and coherence. When similar elements are presented in a consistent manner, readers can more easily grasp the relationships between ideas. For instance, consider the sentence "The company aims to improve productivity, increase efficiency, and reduce costs."

The parallel structure of the verbs "improve," "increase," and "reduce" clearly outlines the company's goals, making the statement more impactful and memorable. Without parallelism, the sentence might become cumbersome and harder to follow. Parallel structure is particularly effective in lists and series, where consistency is crucial for clarity. For example, "The workshop will cover strategies for effective communication, building team cohesion, and fostering innovation." Each item in the list follows the same grammatical pattern, ensuring that the items are perceived as equal and related. In contrast, a non-parallel version like "The workshop will cover strategies for effective communication, how to build team cohesion, and ways to foster innovation" disrupts the rhythm and can confuse readers about the relationship between the items. In addition to lists and series, parallel structure is also important in comparisons and contrasts. For example, "The new policy will benefit employees by offering flexible hours and providing additional training." The parallel structure of the verbs "offering" and "providing" ensures that the benefits are presented in a balanced and clear manner.

Similarly, in comparative sentences, parallelism helps to highlight similarities and differences: "The old system was inefficient and cumbersome, whereas the new system is efficient and user-friendly." When using parallel structure, it is essential to ensure that the elements being compared or listed are of the same grammatical type. For example, "She likes to swim, jogging, and to bike" is not parallel because "swim" and "to bike" are infinitives, while "jogging" is a gerund. A revised, parallel version would be "She likes swimming, jogging, and biking." Maintaining consistent grammatical forms enhances clarity and readability. Parallel structure also plays a crucial role in complex sentences, particularly in the use of correlative conjunctions such as "both...and," "either...or," and "neither...nor." For example, "Both the manager and the assistant are responsible for scheduling meetings" uses parallelism to connect "the manager" and "the assistant" as equal parts of the subject. Similarly, "Either you can attend the meeting or you can submit a written report" maintains parallelism in the verb phrases "attend the meeting" and "submit a written report," ensuring that both options are presented equally. In summary, parallel structure is a powerful tool in writing that enhances clarity, coherence, and readability. By using consistent grammatical forms in lists, comparisons, and complex sentences, writers can create a balanced and organized presentation of ideas. This technique not only improves the overall flow of the text but also helps readers easily understand and retain the information being communicated. Proper use of parallelism contributes to effective writing and ensures that the writer's message is conveyed in a clear and engaging manner.

CHAPTER - 16

COMMON GRAMMAR PITFALLS

16 Introduction

Common grammar pitfalls can significantly undermine the clarity and effectiveness of writing. Understanding and avoiding these mistakes is crucial for producing polished and professional text. Here are some frequent grammar issues to watch out for: Subject-Verb Agreement is a common pitfall where the subject and verb in a sentence must agree in number. Singular subjects require singular verbs, while plural subjects require plural verbs. For instance, "The team are working hard" is incorrect; it should be "The team is working hard." This error often occurs when the subject is collective or when the subject is separated from the verb by other elements in the sentence. Pronoun-Antecedent Agreement is another frequent issue. Pronouns must agree with their antecedents in number, gender, and person.

For example, "Each student should submit their report" is problematic because "each student" is singular, so the correct sentence should be "Each student should submit his or her report." Errors in pronoun-antecedent agreement can confuse readers about who or what is being referred to. Misplaced Modifiers can lead to ambiguous or confusing sentences. Modifiers should be placed next to the word or phrase they are intended to describe. For example, "She nearly drove her kids to school every day" suggests that she almost drove her kids to school, rather than "She drove her kids to school nearly every day." Proper placement ensures that the meaning is clear and unambiguous.

Run-On Sentences occur when two or more independent clauses are incorrectly joined without proper punctuation or conjunctions. For instance, "I went to the store I forgot to buy milk" is a run-on. Correcting it might involve using a period, comma with a conjunction, or a semicolon: "I went to the store, but I forgot to buy milk." Sentence Fragments are incomplete sentences that lack a main clause. They often result from missing subjects or verbs. For example, "Because I was tired" is a fragment because it's an incomplete thought. Adding a main clause, such as "Because I was tired, I went to bed early," corrects the fragment. Comma Splices occur when two independent clauses are joined by a comma without a coordinating conjunction. For example, "I wanted to go to the movies, it was too late" is a comma splice. This can be fixed by using a period, a semicolon, or adding a conjunction: "I wanted to go to the movies, but it was too late."

Incorrect Use of Apostrophes is another common mistake. Apostrophes are used to indicate possession (e.g., "Sarah's book") and to form contractions (e.g., "don't"). However, they should not be used for pluralization (e.g., "The cats are playing" not "The cat's are playing"). Confusing Homophones such as "their," "there," and "they're," or "your" and "you're," can also lead to errors. Understanding the distinct meanings and uses of these words is essential to avoid confusion. For example, "They're going to bring their books over there" uses the correct homophones for "they are," "their," and "there." Dangling Participles occur when a participial phrase does not clearly and logically modify a noun or pronoun. For example, "Walking down the street, the flowers were beautiful" suggests that the flowers were walking, which is incorrect. It should be revised to clarify who was walking: "Walking down the street, I noticed that the flowers were beautiful."

Misuse of Quotation Marks can also be a problem. Quotation marks should enclose exact words spoken or written by someone else. Incorrect use, such as using quotation marks for emphasis, can lead to confusion. For example, "She said she was 'happy' with the results" should be "She said she was happy with the results" if the intention is not to highlight "happy." Inconsistent Tense shifts within a sentence or paragraph can confuse readers. Maintaining consistent verb tense ensures clarity. For instance, "She writes the report and submitted it yesterday" should be corrected to "She wrote the report and submitted it yesterday" to keep the tense consistent. In summary, avoiding common grammar pitfalls involves careful attention to subject-verb agreement, pronoun-antecedent agreement, proper placement of modifiers, correct punctuation, and consistent use of tense and homophones. By being aware of these issues and applying grammatical rules correctly, writers can produce clear, effective, and professional writing.

16.1 Common Mistakes and How to Avoid Them

Common mistakes in writing often stem from misunderstandings or lapses in grammar rules, and addressing these errors is crucial for effective communication. One prevalent mistake is subject-verb agreement, where the subject and verb must match in number. For instance, "The team are playing well" is incorrect; it should be "The team is playing well." To avoid this error, ensure that singular subjects pair with singular verbs and plural subjects with plural verbs, even when intervening words or phrases are present. Pronoun-antecedent agreement is another common issue. Pronouns must agree in number and gender with their antecedents.

For example, "Every student must bring their book" is problematic because "every student" is singular, so it should be "Every student must bring his or her book." To prevent such mistakes, carefully match pronouns with their corresponding nouns in both number and gender. Misplaced modifiers can lead to confusion by creating ambiguous sentences. For instance, "She almost drove her kids to school every day" implies she nearly did so, rather than "She drove her kids to school almost every day." To avoid this, place modifiers next to the words they are meant to describe, ensuring clarity in what is being modified. Run-on sentences occur when two independent clauses are improperly joined without appropriate punctuation. For example, "I went to the store I forgot to buy milk" is a run-on. This can be corrected by using a period, a comma with a conjunction, or a semicolon: "I went to the store, but I forgot to buy milk." Proper punctuation helps to clearly separate ideas and enhance readability.

Sentence fragments are incomplete sentences that lack a main clause. For example, "Because I was tired" is a fragment. To fix this, ensure each sentence includes a subject and a predicate, such as "Because I was tired, I went to bed early." Completing the thought helps maintain grammatical integrity. Comma splices occur when independent clauses are joined by a comma without a conjunction. For example, "I wanted to go to the movies, it was too late" is incorrect. It should be revised to "I wanted to go to the movies, but it was too late" or separated into two sentences. Using the correct punctuation or conjunction avoids this mistake. Incorrect use of apostrophes often confuses possession and contractions. For example, "Its a good day" should be "It's a good day" (contraction of "it is"), while "The cat's toy" correctly shows possession.

To avoid errors, remember that apostrophes indicate possession or contractions, not pluralization. Homophones—words that sound the same but have different meanings—can also be problematic. For instance, "Their" (possessive) vs. "they're" (they are) vs. "there" (place). To avoid confusion, ensure you understand the distinct meanings and uses of homophones, and carefully review your writing for correct usage. Dangling participles occur when a participial phrase does not clearly modify a noun. For example, "Walking down the street, the flowers were beautiful" wrongly suggests that the flowers were walking. A revision like "Walking down the street, I found the flowers beautiful" clarifies the intended meaning and avoids confusion. Inconsistent tense shifts can disrupt the flow and clarity of writing. For example, "She writes the report and submitted it yesterday" mixes present and past tenses. Correct it to "She wrote the report and submitted it yesterday" to maintain tense consistency.

To avoid these common mistakes, rigorous proofreading, a clear understanding of grammatical rules, and careful attention to detail are essential. By addressing these issues, writers can enhance the clarity and professionalism of their text, ensuring effective communication.

16.2 Usage of Commonly Confused Words

Commonly confused words often pose challenges in writing, leading to mistakes that can obscure meaning and hinder communication. Understanding the correct usage of these words is essential for clear and effective writing. For instance, affect and effect are frequently misused. Affect is a verb meaning to influence something, as in "The weather can affect our mood." On the other hand, effect is a noun referring to the result of a change, such as "The new policy had a positive effect on productivity." To avoid confusion, remember that affect usually involves an action, while effect denotes a result. Their, there, and they're are another set of commonly confused words. Their is a possessive adjective indicating ownership, as in "Their house is beautiful." There refers to a place or position, such as "The keys are over there." They're is a contraction for "they are," used in a sentence like "They're planning to visit us next week." Using these words correctly depends on understanding their distinct functions: their for possession, there for location, and they're as a contraction. Your and you're often cause confusion.

Your is a possessive adjective showing something belongs to you, as in "Your report is on the desk." You're is a contraction of "you are," used in sentences like "You're going to enjoy this book." The key to avoiding mistakes is remembering that your indicates possession, while you're refers to the phrase "you are." Its and it's also frequently get mixed up. Its is a possessive adjective referring to something owned by an object or animal, as in "The cat licked its paw." It's is a contraction for "it is" or "it has," as seen in "It's been a long day." To use these words correctly, remember that its shows ownership, and it's is a contraction. Than and then are another pair that can be easily confused. Than is used for comparisons, such as "She is taller than her brother." Then indicates time or sequence, for example, "We went to dinner, and then we watched a movie."

Keeping their distinct uses in mind helps prevent errors: than for comparisons and then for time or sequence. Lose and loose are often mixed up as well. Lose is a verb meaning to misplace or fail to win, as in "I don't want to lose my keys." Loose is an adjective describing something that is not tight, like "The bolt is loose." To avoid mistakes, use lose for actions of misplacing or not winning, and loose for something that isn't tight.

Principal and principle are commonly confused words with different meanings. Principal can refer to a person of authority, such as "The principal of the school addressed the students." It can also denote the main amount of money in finance. Principle refers to a fundamental truth or belief, as in "She adheres to the principle of honesty." Distinguish between them by using principal for people or primary amounts and principle for core truths or rules. Stationary and stationery are another set of words that are often mixed up. Stationary means not moving, as in "The car remained stationary at the red light." Stationery refers to paper and office supplies, such as "I bought new stationery for writing letters." Use stationary to describe something that is not moving and stationery for writing materials. Complement and compliment are also frequently confused. Complement means something that completes or enhances, as in "The wine is a perfect complement to the meal." Compliment is a polite expression of praise, such as "She gave him a compliment on his new suit." To use these correctly, remember that complement enhances something, while compliment involves praise. Finally, desert and dessert are often mixed up. Desert is a dry, arid region, like "The Sahara is a vast desert." Dessert is a sweet course after a meal, as in "We had chocolate cake for dessert." Use desert for arid regions and dessert for sweet treats. By understanding and applying these distinctions, writers can enhance clarity and accuracy in their writing, avoiding common pitfalls associated with these frequently confused words.

CHAPTER - 17

WRITING ESSAYS

17 Introduction of Writing Essays

Writing essays is a fundamental skill that requires clarity, coherence, and a structured approach. The essence of crafting an effective essay lies in its organization and the ability to convey ideas persuasively. An essay typically begins with an introduction, where the writer presents the main topic and provides a thesis statement that outlines the essay's purpose. This section sets the stage for what is to follow, offering a clear preview of the argument or narrative that will be developed. Following the introduction, the body paragraphs constitute the core of the essay. Each paragraph should focus on a specific aspect of the topic, starting with a clear topic sentence that introduces the main idea of that paragraph. Supporting sentences should provide evidence, examples, or detailed explanations that reinforce the topic sentence.

The transitions between paragraphs must be smooth to maintain coherence, guiding the reader through the argument or narrative seamlessly. The strength of the body lies in its ability to present well-organized and relevant information that supports the thesis statement. The conclusion brings closure to the essay by summarizing the key points discussed and restating the thesis in light of the evidence presented. It should also provide a final insight or reflection on the topic, offering a broader perspective or suggesting implications for further consideration. The conclusion is an opportunity to reinforce the significance of the essay's argument and leave a lasting impression on the reader.

Throughout the essay, attention to style and tone is crucial. The language used should be appropriate for the audience and purpose of the essay. Clear, concise writing helps in conveying ideas effectively, while a consistent tone maintains the reader's engagement. Moreover, proper grammar and punctuation are essential for clarity and professionalism. Avoiding common grammatical errors and ensuring that sentences are well-structured enhances the readability of the essay. Revision and editing are integral steps in the essay-writing process. After completing a draft, taking the time to review and refine the content ensures that arguments are well-supported, ideas are clearly articulated, and any errors are corrected. Feedback from peers or instructors can also provide valuable insights for improvement. In summary, writing essays involves a structured approach with a clear introduction, well-organized body paragraphs, and a concise conclusion.

Focusing on style, grammar, and thorough revision enhances the effectiveness of the essay. Mastery of these elements leads to persuasive and well-crafted essays that communicate ideas successfully.

17.1 Structure of an Essay

The structure of an essay is designed to ensure clarity and coherence, allowing the writer to effectively present their ideas and arguments. Here's a breakdown of the typical structure of an essay:

1. Introduction

The introduction serves as the opening of the essay and sets the stage for the reader. It typically includes:

- **Hook**: An engaging opening statement designed to grab the reader's attention. This could be a startling fact, a quote, a question, or an anecdote.

- **Background Information**: Brief context or background on the topic to help the reader understand the subject matter.

- **Thesis Statement**: A clear, concise statement that outlines the main argument or purpose of the essay. It serves as a roadmap for the essay, indicating what the writer intends to prove or discuss.

2. Body Paragraphs

The body of the essay is where the main ideas are developed and supported with evidence. Each body paragraph should include:

- **Topic Sentence**: The first sentence of the paragraph that introduces the main idea or point of that paragraph. It should relate directly to the thesis statement.

- **Supporting Evidence**: Details, examples, facts, or quotations that support the topic sentence and provide evidence for the argument being made.

- **Explanation/Analysis**: Interpretation of the evidence and explanation of how it supports the topic sentence and thesis statement. This section connects the evidence to the overall argument.

- **Transition**: A sentence or phrase that links the current paragraph to the next, ensuring a smooth flow of ideas throughout the essay.

3. Conclusion

The conclusion wraps up the essay and reinforces the main points. It generally includes:

- **Restatement of the Thesis**: A rephrased version of the thesis statement, reflecting how the essay has addressed the topic.

- **Summary of Main Points**: A brief overview of the key arguments or findings presented in the body paragraphs.
- **Closing Thought**: A final insight, reflection, or call to action. This might involve suggesting implications, posing a rhetorical question, or providing a broader perspective on the topic.

4. Additional Elements

Depending on the type of essay, additional elements might include:

- **Introduction to Counterarguments**: In argumentative essays, acknowledging and addressing opposing views can strengthen the argument.
- **Recommendations or Future Directions**: In essays discussing research or policy, offering recommendations or suggesting future areas for study can be relevant.

By adhering to this structure, writers can ensure that their essays are well-organized, logically coherent, and effectively communicate their ideas to the reader.

17.2 Thesis Statements

A thesis statement is a fundamental element of an essay that encapsulates the central argument or main point the writer aims to communicate. It functions as a guiding beacon for both the writer and the reader, setting the direction and focus of the essay. Typically located at the end of the introduction paragraph, the thesis statement serves several crucial roles in an effective essay. Firstly, the thesis statement provides a clear and concise summary of the essay's main argument or claim. It distills the essence of what the writer intends to discuss and prove, offering a snapshot of the essay's purpose. For instance, in an essay exploring the impacts of technology on education, a well-defined thesis might be, "While technology has revolutionized educational practices and access, it has also introduced challenges such as digital distraction and inequity." This statement clearly outlines the dual nature of the argument, setting up a framework for discussing both positive and negative aspects of the topic. Secondly, the thesis statement establishes the scope of the essay.

It defines the specific focus of the discussion, ensuring that the writer stays on track and that the content remains relevant to the central argument. A precise thesis statement helps prevent the essay from becoming too broad or deviating from the main point. For example, "The integration of artificial intelligence in the classroom enhances personalized learning but raises concerns about data privacy and ethical use" narrows the focus to two key areas: personalized learning and ethical issues, guiding the structure of the body paragraphs. Moreover, a strong thesis statement should be debatable and provoke thought. It is not merely a statement of fact but rather an assertion that invites analysis and discussion. It should present a viewpoint or argument that requires evidence and reasoning to support. For example, "Government policies aimed at reducing carbon emissions are essential for combating climate change, but they must be paired with comprehensive international cooperation to be effective" suggests a position that can be supported with evidence and explored in depth, rather than a simple, non-controversial fact.

The thesis statement also serves as a tool for engaging the reader. A well-crafted thesis piques the reader's interest by presenting a compelling argument or perspective. It sets the stage for the essay's discussion, creating anticipation for how the argument will be developed. For instance, "While many argue that urbanization leads to economic growth, it is crucial to examine its effects on social inequality and environmental degradation" offers a thought-provoking perspective that invites the reader to explore a nuanced discussion. In constructing a thesis statement, it is important to ensure that it is clear, specific, and assertive. Avoid vague language or overly broad statements that do not provide a clear direction for the essay. Instead, aim for a thesis that succinctly conveys the main argument and outlines the key points that will be discussed. In summary, the thesis statement is a vital component of an essay, providing a clear summary of the main argument, defining the scope, offering a debatable claim, and engaging the reader. By crafting a precise and compelling thesis statement, writers can effectively guide their essays and ensure that their arguments are coherent and focused.

17.3 Supporting Arguments

Supporting arguments are crucial elements in an essay, as they provide the evidence and reasoning needed to substantiate the thesis statement. Each supporting argument is designed to reinforce the central claim by offering detailed explanations, examples, and evidence that validate the writer's viewpoint.

These arguments are typically presented in the body paragraphs of the essay, with each paragraph dedicated to a specific point that contributes to the overall argument. To effectively support an argument, it is essential to present clear, relevant evidence. This might include statistical data, research findings, historical examples, or real-life anecdotes. For example, if the thesis statement argues that renewable energy sources are crucial for sustainable development, supporting arguments could include data showing the reduction in greenhouse gas emissions from renewable energy, examples of successful renewable energy projects, and expert opinions on the long-term benefits of such technologies. In addition to providing evidence, supporting arguments should include thorough analysis and explanation. This means not only presenting facts but also interpreting their significance and showing how they relate to the thesis statement. It is important to explain how each piece of evidence strengthens the argument, clarifies complex ideas, or addresses potential counterarguments.

For instance, if discussing the economic advantages of renewable energy, one should analyze how the creation of green jobs and energy independence contribute to economic stability, thereby supporting the overall claim. Furthermore, each supporting argument should be well-organized and logically structured. This involves presenting arguments in a coherent order, using transition sentences to connect ideas, and ensuring that each paragraph focuses on a single aspect of the thesis. Clear and concise writing helps in maintaining focus and making the argument persuasive. For example, when discussing various benefits of renewable energy, a writer might structure paragraphs around different benefits such as environmental impact, economic growth, and technological innovation, ensuring that each paragraph builds on the previous one and contributes to the overall argument. In summary, supporting arguments are essential for substantiating the thesis statement in an essay. They involve presenting relevant evidence, providing detailed analysis, and ensuring logical organization. By effectively developing and presenting supporting arguments, writers can strengthen their essays and persuasively convey their main points.

17.4 Conclusion

The conclusion of an essay serves as the final opportunity to reinforce the main argument and leave a lasting impression on the reader. It should succinctly summarize the key points discussed in the body paragraphs, reaffirming how they support the thesis statement. This recap helps to remind the reader of the essay's central arguments and demonstrates how the evidence and analysis presented throughout the essay converge to validate the main claim.

A well-crafted conclusion also offers a broader perspective or insight, reflecting on the significance of the argument or suggesting implications for future consideration. For instance, if the essay discussed the impact of renewable energy on environmental sustainability, the conclusion might emphasize the critical role of continued investment in green technologies and the need for global cooperation to address climate change effectively. By tying together the main points and offering a reflective or forward-looking statement, the conclusion not only reinforces the essay's message but also encourages the reader to contemplate the broader relevance of the topic.

CHAPTER - 18

CREATIVE WRITING

18. Introduction of Creative Writing

Creative writing is an art form that goes beyond mere storytelling to explore the depths of imagination and emotion. It encompasses a broad range of genres, including fiction, poetry, and drama, each with its own unique style and techniques. The essence of creative writing lies in its ability to captivate the reader through compelling narratives, vivid imagery, and innovative language use. Unlike technical or academic writing, which prioritizes clarity and precision, creative writing embraces the freedom to experiment with language, structure, and form. At the heart of creative writing is character development, which involves creating complex, believable characters with distinct personalities, motivations, and growth arcs.

Writers use various techniques to bring characters to life, such as detailed descriptions, internal monologues, and dynamic interactions with other characters. For example, in a novel, a writer might depict a character's inner struggles through stream-of-consciousness narration, revealing their fears, desires, and conflicts in a way that resonates deeply with readers. Another crucial element is plot construction, which involves crafting a series of events that engage the reader and drive the narrative forward. A well-developed plot includes an engaging beginning that introduces the setting and conflict, a middle that builds tension and develops the story, and a satisfying resolution that concludes the narrative arc. Creative writers often employ various techniques to enhance their plots, such as foreshadowing, flashbacks, and non-linear storytelling.

For instance, a writer might use flashbacks to reveal a character's backstory, adding depth and complexity to the narrative. Setting plays a significant role in creative writing, providing the backdrop against which the story unfolds. A vivid, well-described setting can enhance the mood, create atmosphere, and contribute to the story's themes. Writers use sensory details and descriptive language to immerse readers in the world of the story, making the setting feel tangible and real. Whether it's a bustling city, a serene countryside, or a fantastical realm, the setting can significantly influence the story's tone and impact. Dialogue is another key component of creative writing, as it reveals character relationships, advances the plot, and adds authenticity to the narrative. Effective dialogue should sound natural and reflect each character's unique voice and personality.

Writers craft dialogue to convey emotions, conflicts, and dynamics between characters, making interactions feel genuine and engaging. For instance, sharp, witty exchanges between characters can highlight their personalities and build tension, while introspective conversations can reveal deeper themes and motivations. Moreover, language and style in creative writing are vital for crafting an engaging and memorable narrative. Writers experiment with word choice, sentence structure, and literary devices such as metaphors, similes, and imagery to create a distinct voice and evoke specific emotions. The style can range from lyrical and poetic to terse and minimalist, depending on the story's tone and genre. For example, a poetic description of a sunset can evoke a sense of tranquility and wonder, while a stark, concise narrative might create a feeling of urgency or tension. In essence, creative writing is about exploring human experiences and emotions through imaginative and expressive means. It invites writers to push the boundaries of conventional language and storytelling, crafting narratives that resonate with readers on a deeper level. By focusing on character development, plot construction, setting, dialogue, and stylistic elements, creative writers can create compelling and immersive stories that captivate and inspire.

18.1 Writing Narratives

Writing narratives involves crafting stories that captivate readers through engaging plots, vivid settings, and well-developed characters. At its core, narrative writing is about creating a coherent and compelling sequence of events that unfolds in a structured manner. It begins with a clear introduction that sets the scene, introduces the main characters, and establishes the initial conflict or situation. This setup is crucial for drawing readers into the story and providing them with the context they need to understand the subsequent events. As the narrative progresses, the body of the story develops through a series of events that build tension and advance the plot. This part of the narrative is characterized by the rising action, where conflicts and complications arise, challenging the characters and propelling the story forward. Effective narratives often include moments of climax, where the tension reaches its peak, and the protagonist faces a critical decision or turning point. This is followed by the falling action, where the consequences of the climax are addressed, leading to the story's resolution. Character development is a key element in narrative writing. Characters should be well-rounded and dynamic, exhibiting growth and change throughout the story. Writers achieve this by showing characters' thoughts, emotions, and interactions, allowing readers to connect with them on a deeper level. For example, a protagonist might start with certain flaws or challenges but evolve through their experiences, demonstrating growth by the end of the narrative.

The setting also plays a significant role in narrative writing, providing the backdrop against which the story unfolds. A well-described setting enhances the mood and atmosphere, helping readers visualize the environment and understand its influence on the characters and plot. Whether it's a bustling city, a quiet village, or a fantastical world, the setting should be described with enough detail to make it feel real and immersive. Dialogue is another crucial aspect of narrative writing. Authentic and meaningful dialogue reveals character traits, advances the plot, and adds realism to the story. It should reflect each character's unique voice and personality, contributing to the overall development of the narrative. Through dialogue, writers can also convey emotions, conflicts, and relationships, making interactions between characters feel genuine and engaging. Point of view is an important narrative choice that influences how the story is presented to the reader. Whether told from a first-person perspective, where the narrator is a character in the story, or a third-person perspective, where the narrator is outside the story, the chosen point of view affects how much the reader knows about the characters and events. Writers must be consistent with their point of view and use it effectively to control the flow of information and emotional impact. In summary, writing narratives involves weaving together characters, plot, setting, and dialogue to create a compelling and coherent story. By focusing on these elements and crafting them thoughtfully, writers can engage readers and bring their stories to life.

18.2 Writing Descriptive Pieces

A descriptive piece of writing focuses on painting vivid and detailed pictures through words, immersing the reader in a sensory experience. Unlike narrative writing, which emphasizes plot and character development, descriptive writing centers on the intricate portrayal of people, places, objects, or events. The goal is to evoke a strong sense of atmosphere and mood by appealing to the reader's senses—sight, sound, smell, taste, and touch. In a descriptive piece, the writer uses rich, evocative language to create a clear and immersive image in the reader's mind. This often involves detailed observations and carefully chosen adjectives and adverbs that bring the subject to life. For example, instead of merely stating "the garden was beautiful," a descriptive piece might elaborate, "The garden was a riot of color, with vibrant tulips and daffodils swaying gently in the breeze, their petals glistening with morning dew under the warm, golden sunlight." This approach not only provides a vivid image but also conveys the feeling and atmosphere of the scene. Effective descriptive writing also utilizes figurative language, such as metaphors, similes, and personification, to add depth and dimension.

For instance, comparing the rustling leaves to "a whispering conversation" or describing a storm as "nature's fury unleashed" enhances the sensory experience and engages the reader's imagination. In addition to visual details, a descriptive piece might include sensory descriptions that evoke sound, smell, taste, and touch. For instance, describing the aroma of freshly baked bread or the texture of a rough, weathered surface adds layers to the depiction and enriches the reader's engagement with the text. The writer's choice of words and the level of detail are crucial, as they help to create a compelling and immersive experience that transports the reader to the scene being described. Ultimately, a descriptive piece aims to provide readers with a profound sense of what it is like to experience the described subject. It requires careful observation and thoughtful word choice to effectively convey the nuances and subtleties of the scene, object, or person. By focusing on the sensory details and using evocative language, descriptive writing creates a vivid and memorable impression that enhances the reader's connection to the text.

CHAPTER - 19

FORMAL WRITING

19 Introduction of Formal Writing

Formal writing is a style of communication characterized by its adherence to specific conventions, tone, and structure, aimed at conveying information clearly, professionally, and respectfully. It is typically used in academic, business, and professional settings where clarity, precision, and a respectful tone are crucial. The primary goal of formal writing is to present ideas and arguments in a manner that is objective, well-organized, and free from colloquial language and personal biases. In formal writing, tone plays a significant role. The tone should be professional and objective, avoiding casual language or personal opinions. This means using precise vocabulary and maintaining a respectful distance from the subject matter. For instance, instead of using contractions like "don't" or "can't," formal writing prefers "do not" and "cannot."

Additionally, formal writing often employs a third-person perspective, which helps to maintain objectivity and avoids the personal biases that might come with a first-person viewpoint. Structure is another essential element of formal writing. It follows a clear and logical organization that typically includes an introduction, body, and conclusion. The introduction sets the context for the topic and presents the thesis statement or main argument. The body of the text is divided into paragraphs, each of which focuses on a specific point or piece of evidence supporting the thesis. These paragraphs are usually structured with a topic sentence, supporting details, and a concluding sentence. The conclusion summarizes the main points, reiterates the thesis, and may suggest implications or future directions.

This structure ensures that the content is organized and that the argument is developed in a coherent manner. Clarity and precision are crucial in formal writing. Writers are expected to use specific, accurate language and avoid ambiguity. This involves choosing words carefully to convey exact meanings and using technical or academic terms appropriately. For example, in a research paper, a writer would use precise terminology related to the field of study and provide clear definitions when necessary. Avoiding vague language helps to ensure that the reader fully understands the writer's points and arguments. Evidence and support are also key components of formal writing. Arguments and claims should be backed by credible sources and well-reasoned evidence.

This includes citing academic research, statistical data, or expert opinions to substantiate the points made. Proper citation not only lends credibility to the writing but also acknowledges the work of others, adhering to academic integrity standards. Additionally, formal writing adheres to specific grammatical and stylistic conventions. This includes using complete sentences, proper punctuation, and a consistent format. For instance, in business writing, formal letters follow a standard format with clear sections such as the sender's address, date, recipient's address, salutation, body, and closing. Maintaining grammatical accuracy and following stylistic guidelines helps to enhance the professionalism of the writing and ensures that it meets the expectations of its intended audience. Avoiding informal language and personal anecdotes is another hallmark of formal writing.

Instead, the focus is on factual information and logical reasoning. Expressions of personal opinions or informal language, such as slang or colloquialisms, are typically avoided to maintain a professional tone. For example, rather than saying "the project was a huge success," a formal writer might state "the project achieved its objectives and demonstrated significant results." In summary, formal writing is characterized by its adherence to a professional tone, clear structure, and precise language. It requires careful organization, objective reasoning, and adherence to grammatical conventions to effectively communicate ideas in academic, business, and professional contexts. By focusing on clarity, evidence, and a respectful tone, formal writing ensures that the content is presented in a manner that is both authoritative and accessible to its intended audience.

.1 Writing Letters

Writing letters involves crafting messages that convey information, requests, or sentiments in a clear and structured manner. Whether formal or informal, letters follow a specific format and tone depending on their purpose and audience. Formal letters are used in professional, academic, or official contexts and require a specific structure to ensure clarity and professionalism.

1. The format typically includes:

- Sender's Address: Placed at the top right corner of the page. This includes the writer's full address.

- Date: Written below the sender's address, indicating when the letter was composed.

- Recipient's Address: Positioned on the left side of the page, just below the date. This includes the recipient's name, title, and address.

- Salutation: A formal greeting addressing the recipient. Common examples include "Dear Mr. Smith" or "Dear Dr. Johnson." If the recipient's gender is unknown, "Dear Sir or Madam" is used.

- Body: The main content of the letter, usually divided into paragraphs. The first paragraph typically introduces the purpose of the letter, followed by detailed information or requests, and a concluding paragraph summarizing or reiterating the main point.

- Closing: A formal sign-off such as "Sincerely," "Yours faithfully," or "Best regards." This is followed by a comma.

- Signature: The writer's name, with a handwritten signature above it if the letter is printed. For electronic letters, a typed signature is acceptable.

For example, a formal letter requesting a meeting might begin with a salutation like "Dear Ms. Taylor," followed by a clear introduction stating the purpose of the letter, such as discussing a project. The body would provide details about the proposed meeting and any relevant background information, concluding with a polite request to schedule a time. The closing would be something like "Sincerely," followed by the writer's name. Informal letters, on the other hand, are used for personal communication and can be more relaxed in tone and structure.

2. **They typically include:**

- Date: Positioned at the top left or right corner.

- Salutation: Often more casual, such as "Hi John" or "Dear Jane."

- Body: This section is less structured and can be conversational, covering personal updates, thoughts, or stories. It is usually written in a more relaxed style compared to formal letters.

- Closing: Informal sign-offs like "Best wishes," "Love," or "Cheers," followed by a comma.

- Signature: The writer's name, which can be followed by a personal note or nickname.

For instance, an informal letter to a friend might start with "Dear Sarah," followed by a friendly update about recent events in the writer's life, and conclude with a warm closing such as "Love," followed by the writer's name. In both types of letters, clarity and appropriateness are essential. Formal letters should adhere to professional norms and be free from errors, while informal letters should reflect the writer's personal voice and relationship with the recipient. By following the appropriate format and tone for the intended audience, writers can effectively communicate their messages and maintain the intended level of professionalism or intimacy.

.2 Writing Reports

Writing reports involves creating structured documents that convey information, analysis, or recommendations on a specific topic or issue. Reports are typically used in professional, academic, or business contexts to present findings, track progress, or make informed decisions. The structure and content of a report can vary depending on its purpose, audience, and type, but most reports follow a general framework that ensures clarity and comprehensiveness.

1. **Title Page**: The title page provides essential information about the report. It includes the report title, the author's name, the date of completion, and any relevant institutional or organizational details. A well-crafted title should clearly reflect the report's content and

purpose.

2. **Table of Contents**: This section lists the main headings and subheadings of the report, along with their corresponding page numbers. It helps readers quickly locate specific sections of the report and understand its structure.

3. **Executive Summary or Abstract**: The executive summary (for business reports) or abstract (for academic reports) offers a concise overview of the report's main findings, conclusions, and recommendations. It is typically written after the report is completed and should summarize the key points in a way that allows readers to grasp the essence of the report without reading the entire document.

4. **Introduction**: The introduction sets the stage for the report by outlining the purpose, scope, and objectives. It provides background information on the topic, explains why the report is being written, and describes the methodology used for gathering and analyzing data.

5. **Methodology**: This section details the methods and procedures used to collect and analyze data. It includes information on research design, data sources, sampling techniques, and any tools or instruments used. The methodology should be clear and replicable, allowing readers to understand how the findings were obtained.

6. **Findings or Results**: In this section, the report presents the data and information collected during the research or investigation. It includes detailed descriptions, tables, charts, and graphs to illustrate the findings. The presentation of results should be objective and factual, with careful attention to accuracy and clarity.

7. **Discussion**: The discussion interprets the findings, analyzing their implications and significance. It relates the results to the report's objectives and provides insights into their meaning. This section may also address any limitations or potential sources of error in the study.

8. **Conclusion**: The conclusion summarizes the main points of the report and draws final conclusions based on the findings and discussion. It reiterates the significance of the results and provides a clear summary of what has been learned from the report.

9. **Recommendations**: Based on the findings and conclusions, this section offers specific, actionable suggestions or solutions. Recommendations should be practical and feasible, providing clear guidance for addressing the issues identified in the report.

10. **References or Bibliography**: This section lists all the sources cited or consulted in the preparation of the report. It provides full details of books, articles, websites, and other materials used, following a specific citation style (such as APA, MLA, or Chicago).

11. **Appendices**: Appendices include supplementary materials that support the report but are too detailed or lengthy to include in the main sections. This might include raw data, additional charts or graphs, or detailed explanations of methodologies. Appendices are referenced in the main text but are placed at the end of the report.

.3   Tips for Effective Report Writing:

- Clarity: Use clear and precise language. Avoid jargon unless it is necessary and ensure that technical terms are defined.

- Structure: Follow a logical structure to help readers navigate the report. Use headings and subheadings to organize content.

- Accuracy: Ensure that all data and information presented are accurate and properly verified.

- Objectivity: Maintain an objective tone throughout the report, focusing on facts and evidence rather than personal opinions.

- Proofreading: Review the report for grammatical errors, inconsistencies, and formatting issues before finalizing.

In summary, writing a report involves a systematic approach to presenting information, analysis, and recommendations. By following a structured format and focusing on clarity, accuracy, and objectivity, writers can create effective reports that serve their intended purpose and communicate their findings effectively.

CHAPTER - 20

GRAMMAR IN SPOKEN ENGLISH

20 Introduction of Spoken English

Grammar in spoken English plays a critical role in ensuring clear and effective communication, even though it often differs from the formal rules observed in written English. In everyday conversation, grammar is more flexible and adaptive to the natural flow of speech, reflecting the dynamic nature of verbal interaction. This flexibility allows speakers to communicate efficiently without adhering strictly to formal grammatical rules, but a basic understanding of grammatical principles can still enhance clarity and prevent misunderstandings. Sentence structure in spoken English often deviates from traditional written forms. Spoken sentences are usually shorter and simpler, and it's common to encounter fragments or incomplete sentences that are understood through context. For instance, instead of constructing a complete sentence such as "I would like to go to the store," a speaker might simply say "Going to the store?"

The listener can still understand the intended meaning due to the conversational context. Verb tense in spoken English also exhibits a degree of flexibility. While precise tense usage is crucial in written English to indicate the exact timing of actions, spoken English often relies on context and temporal markers like "yesterday" or "soon" to convey when events occur. For example, in a conversation, a speaker might say "I see him yesterday" instead of the grammatically correct

"I saw him yesterday," and the meaning remains clear due to contextual clues. Pronouns and their antecedents can sometimes be less strictly managed in spoken English. In rapid conversation, speakers may omit pronouns or use them loosely, depending on how well the listener can infer the subject from the context.

For instance, a speaker might say, "Told him to call," where "I told him to call" would be the complete form in written English. The context usually makes the meaning clear. Use of contractions is prevalent in spoken English, contributing to a more natural and fluid conversational style. Contractions like "don't," "can't," "won't," and "isn't" are commonly used to streamline speech and make it sound more informal and conversational. This is in contrast to the more formal and complete expressions often used in writing. Questions and negations in spoken English may also differ from their written counterparts. In casual speech, the formation of questions and negations can be more relaxed. For example, instead of asking, "Are you going to the party?" one might say, "You going to the party?"

Similarly, negations may be formed using informal structures such as "I don't know nothing" instead of the grammatically correct "I don't know anything." Colloquial language and idiomatic expressions frequently appear in spoken English, adding richness and color to conversations but often straying from formal grammatical rules. Expressions like "gonna" for "going to" or "wanna" for "want to" are commonly used in informal speech. These idiomatic forms may not adhere strictly to traditional grammar rules but are widely understood in everyday conversation In summary, grammar in spoken English exhibits a level of flexibility that accommodates the natural rhythm and immediacy of verbal communication. While it often deviates from formal written standards, a basic grasp of grammatical principles helps in crafting clear and effective speech. Understanding how sentence structure, verb tense, pronouns, contractions, and colloquial expressions function in conversation can enhance clarity and ensure that spoken communication is both comprehensible and contextually appropriate.

20.1 Formal vs. Informal Speech

Formal versus informal speech represents two distinct styles of communication that serve different purposes and contexts. Understanding the differences between them is crucial for effective interaction in various settings, from professional environments to casual conversations. Formal speech is characterized by its adherence to established rules and conventions. It is typically used in professional, academic, or official contexts where clarity, precision, and respect are paramount. This style of speech often includes:

• Structured Language: Formal speech employs complete sentences and follows grammatical rules more strictly. For example, instead of saying, "I'm gonna send the report," a formal tone would use, "I am going to send the report."

• Polite and Respectful Tone: Formal speech often includes polite expressions and titles, such as "Mr.," "Ms.," "Dr.," and "Professor." It avoids slang and colloquial language, opting instead for more neutral and respectful phrasing. For instance, one might say, "Could you please provide the necessary information?" rather than "Can you give me the info?"

• Complex Sentence Structures: In formal speech, sentences are often more complex, incorporating subordinate clauses and precise vocabulary to convey detailed information. This structure helps in articulating arguments or explanations clearly and comprehensively.

- Avoidance of Contractions: Formal speech generally avoids contractions, using the full forms of words. For example, "cannot" is preferred over "can't," and "do not" is preferred over "don't." This contributes to a more polished and professional tone.

- Objective Language: The language in formal speech is usually objective and impartial, focusing on facts and evidence rather than personal opinions or emotions. This helps maintain a professional and neutral stance.

Informal speech, on the other hand, is used in casual or familiar settings and is characterized by its relaxed and conversational tone. Key features of informal speech include:

- Casual Language: Informal speech often includes contractions and colloquial expressions. Phrases like "gonna" for "going to" and "wanna" for "want to" are common. Informal speech may also incorporate slang or idioms, such as "cool" or "piece of cake."

- Relaxed Grammar: In informal speech, grammatical rules can be more flexible. Sentence fragments and run-on sentences are more acceptable, as conversations are often spontaneous and less structured. For instance, one might say, "I was like, 'What's up?'" instead of, "I said, 'What's up?'"

- Familiar Tone: Informal speech is characterized by a friendly and relaxed tone. It may include direct address and personal pronouns, such as "you" and "I," and often features a conversational style. For example, "Hey, how's it going?" is a common informal greeting.

- Shorter Sentences: Sentences in informal speech are often

shorter and simpler, designed to facilitate quick and efficient communication. This is especially useful in everyday interactions where brevity and clarity are needed.

- **Personal Touch:** Informal speech may involve personal anecdotes, emotional expressions, and humor. This style helps to create a sense of intimacy and connection between speakers, making it suitable for social interactions and casual conversations.

In summary, formal and informal speech serve different purposes and contexts. Formal speech is characterized by its adherence to grammatical rules, polite tone, and structured language, making it suitable for professional and academic settings. Informal speech, with its casual language, relaxed grammar, and personal touch, is more appropriate for everyday conversations and social interactions.

Understanding when and how to use each style effectively can enhance communication and ensure that interactions are appropriate for the context.

20.2 Common Spoken Grammar Errors

Common spoken grammar errors are frequent issues that arise in everyday conversations due to the informal nature of spoken language. These errors can affect clarity and comprehension but are often tolerated in casual settings. However, understanding and correcting these mistakes can improve communication skills and help in various social and professional contexts.

- **Misuse of Verb Tenses:** In spoken English, it is common to see errors in verb tense usage. For instance, speakers might say, "I seen him yesterday" instead of the correct "I saw him yesterday." The use of the incorrect past tense form can lead to confusion about when an event occurred.

- **Subject-Verb Agreement Errors**: A common issue in spoken English is the mismatch between subjects and verbs. For example, saying "She don't know the answer" instead of "She doesn't know the answer" is a frequent error. This mistake often occurs when the subject and verb do not agree in number or person.

- **Sentence Fragments**: Spoken language often includes incomplete sentences or fragments that may lack a subject or predicate. For instance, someone might say, "Because I was late" without completing the thought. While these fragments are usually understood in context, they can lead to confusion if the context is unclear.

- **Misplaced or Missing Pronouns**: Pronouns may be used incorrectly or omitted in spoken language. For example, "Him and me went to the store" instead of "He and I went to the store" is a common error. This mistake can affect the clarity of who is being referred to and how the sentence is constructed.

- **Incorrect Use of Contractions**: In informal speech, contractions are common, but incorrect usage can occur. For instance, "They should of known better" instead of "They should have known better" is an error where the contraction is confused with the incorrect form "of" instead of "have."

- **Double Negatives**: Double negatives are often used in spoken English but can lead to confusion. For example, "I don't need no help" should be "I don't need any help." The use of double negatives can sometimes unintentionally create a positive meaning, altering the intended message.

- **Overuse of Fillers**: Spoken language frequently includes fillers like "um," "uh," "like," and "you know." While these fillers are natural in conversation, excessive use can detract from the clarity and effectiveness of speech. They can also make the speaker appear less confident or less prepared.

- **Run-On Sentences**: In spoken English, run-on sentences are common, where multiple independent clauses are joined without proper punctuation. For example, "I went to the store and I bought milk and then I went home" is a run-on sentence that could be clearer if broken into separate sentences or properly punctuated.

- **Incorrect Word Order**: The order of words in a sentence can sometimes be incorrect in spoken English. For instance, saying "Can you me help?" instead of "Can you help me?" disrupts the natural flow and structure of the sentence.

- **Mispronunciations and Slang**: While not strictly a grammatical error, mispronunciations and the use of slang can affect the clarity of spoken communication. For example, saying "aks" instead of "ask" can lead to misunderstandings, and excessive use of regional slang may not be understood by all listeners.

In summary, common spoken grammar errors include issues with verb tenses, subject-verb agreement, sentence fragments, pronoun usage, contractions, double negatives, fillers, run-on sentences, word order, and mispronunciations. While these errors are natural in everyday conversation, being aware of them and making an effort to correct them can enhance clarity and effectiveness in communication.

CHAPTER - 21

PROOFREADING AND EDITING

21 Introduction of Proofreading

Proofreading and editing are essential processes in refining written content to ensure clarity, coherence, and correctness. Though often used interchangeably, they serve distinct purposes and involve different strategies to improve a document's quality. Proofreading is the final step in the writing process, focusing on surface-level errors. This stage involves meticulously reviewing the text to correct issues such as spelling mistakes, grammatical errors, punctuation errors, and formatting inconsistencies. The goal of proofreading is to ensure that the document is free from typographical errors and adheres to the required style guide. Effective proofreading requires attention to detail and a thorough reading of the text, often multiple times.

Tools such as spell checkers can assist, but human review is crucial as these tools may miss contextual errors or nuances. Editing, on the other hand, is a broader process that occurs before proofreading. It involves a more in-depth review of the text to improve its overall structure, flow, and readability. Editing includes checking for clarity, coherence, and consistency in the content. It involves reorganizing paragraphs, refining sentence structures, and ensuring that ideas are logically presented and well-supported. Editors look at the big picture, addressing issues such as redundant information, awkward phrasing, and inconsistencies in tone or style.

Editing may also involve verifying facts and ensuring that the document meets its intended purpose and audience.

The editing process typically involves several key steps. Initially, the editor reviews the overall structure of the document to ensure that it follows a logical progression. This includes checking the introduction, body, and conclusion for cohesion and coherence. The next step involves refining the language used, improving clarity and readability by eliminating jargon or complex sentence structures. Additionally, editors pay attention to consistency in terms of style, tone, and formatting, ensuring that the document adheres to any specific guidelines or standards. Proofreading is usually the final step after editing, focusing on catching any remaining errors that might have been overlooked. This includes reviewing the document for spelling and grammatical mistakes, checking punctuation, and ensuring consistent formatting. Proofreaders often use techniques such as reading the text aloud, which helps to catch errors that may not be apparent when reading silently.

They also look for typographical errors and ensure that all references and citations are correctly formatted. Both proofreading and editing require a critical eye and a systematic approach. It's often helpful to take breaks between editing and proofreading sessions to gain fresh perspectives on the text. Additionally, utilizing tools like grammar checkers and style guides can aid in the process, but they should complement, not replace, careful manual review.

In summary, proofreading and editing are crucial steps in producing polished and professional written content. Proofreading focuses on correcting surface-level errors such as spelling and punctuation, while editing involves a more comprehensive review of structure, clarity, and style. Both processes contribute to enhancing the readability and effectiveness of the document, ensuring that it meets the desired standards and communicates its message effectively.

21.1 Tips for Effective Proofreading

Effective proofreading is crucial for ensuring that a document is free from errors and presents information clearly and professionally. Here are several tips to enhance your proofreading skills:

- Firstly, take a break before proofreading. After completing a draft, stepping away from the document for a short period can help you return with a fresh perspective, making it easier to spot mistakes that might have been overlooked during initial writing.

- Secondly, read the document aloud. This technique helps in catching errors that you might not notice when reading silently. Hearing the text can reveal awkward phrasing, run-on sentences, and grammatical issues more effectively.

- Additionally, proofread in multiple passes. Focus on different types of errors in each pass—one for spelling and grammar, another for punctuation, and a third for formatting and consistency. This segmented approach can help you catch a wider range of issues.

- Use digital tools as aids, but don't rely solely on them. Grammar and spell checkers can identify many errors, but they may miss contextual mistakes or suggest incorrect changes. Combining these tools with manual proofreading ensures a more thorough review.

- Print out the document if possible. Reading a physical copy can help you notice errors that are easily missed on a screen. Changes in format and the act of handling the paper can also aid in spotting issues.

- Focus on one type of error at a time. For instance, first check for spelling mistakes, then for punctuation errors, and finally for formatting inconsistencies. This focused approach prevents you from getting overwhelmed and improves the accuracy of your proofreading.

- Use a ruler or a finger to guide your eyes line by line. This technique helps maintain focus and prevents you from skipping lines or missing errors due to visual fatigue.

- Check for consistency in formatting, style, and terminology throughout the document. Ensure that headings, fonts, and citations are uniformly applied, and verify that terms and names are used consistently.

- Pay attention to commonly confused words. Words like "their," "there," and "they're" or "affect" and "effect" can easily be mistaken for one another, so be diligent in checking their correct usage.

- Lastly, ask someone else to review the document. A fresh set of eyes can catch mistakes you might have missed and provide valuable feedback on the overall clarity and coherence of the text.

By employing these tips, you can enhance your proofreading process, ensuring that your document is polished, professional, and error-free.

21.2 Common Errors to Look For

Common errors to look for during proofreading are crucial for ensuring that a document is clear, accurate, and professional. Addressing these issues can significantly improve the quality of writing and prevent miscommunication. Here are key areas to focus on:

- **Spelling Mistakes**: Misspelled words are among the most frequent errors. While spell checkers can catch many of these, they may not always identify homophones (e.g., "their" vs. "there") or context-specific errors. Carefully review each word, particularly those that are often confused or subject to frequent typographical errors.

- **Grammar Issues**: Grammar errors can disrupt the flow and clarity of the text. Common issues include incorrect verb tenses, subject-verb agreement errors, and improper use of articles. For example, "She don't like coffee" should be "She doesn't like coffee." Make sure that verbs agree with their subjects in number and tense and that articles ("a," "an," "the") are used appropriately.

- **Punctuation Errors**: Proper punctuation is vital for readability. Look for missing or misplaced commas, periods, semicolons, and other punctuation marks.

For instance, missing commas can lead to run-on sentences, while misplaced semicolons can confuse the reader. Ensure that commas are used to separate clauses and list items correctly, and check that periods and other end punctuation marks are appropriately placed.

- **Sentence Fragments**: Sentence fragments are incomplete sentences that lack a subject or predicate, making them grammatically incorrect. These often occur in casual writing but need correction in formal documents. For example, "Although I was late" is a fragment that should be completed with "Although I was late, I still attended the meeting."

- **Run-On Sentences**: Run-on sentences occur when two or more independent clauses are joined without proper punctuation or conjunctions. For example, "I went to the store I bought milk" should be corrected to "I went to the store, and I bought milk." Use commas, semicolons, or conjunctions to separate independent clauses properly.

- **Misuse of Pronouns**: Pronouns must agree with their antecedents in number and gender. Errors occur when pronouns are incorrectly used or when their antecedents are unclear. For instance, "Everyone should bring their own pencil" might be clearer as "Everyone should bring his or her own pencil," although context often allows for a more natural solution like "Everyone should bring their own pencil."

- **Consistency Issues**: Consistency is essential in any document, especially in terms of style, terminology, and formatting. Check for uniformity in the use of fonts, headings, bullet points, and numbering. Ensure that terminology is consistent throughout the document to avoid confusion.

- **Incorrect Word Choice**: Selecting the wrong word or using a word inappropriately can alter the meaning of a sentence. Watch for words that are commonly confused or misused, such as "affect" vs. "effect" or "accept" vs. "except." Verify that the chosen words convey the intended meaning accurately.

- **Misplaced Modifiers**: Modifiers should be placed next to the words they modify to avoid ambiguity. Misplaced modifiers can lead to confusing or incorrect sentences. For example, "She almost drove her kids to school every day" should be "She drove her kids to school almost every day" to convey the intended meaning accurately.

- **Formatting Errors**: Formatting consistency is crucial for a professional appearance. Look for inconsistencies in font size, style, and spacing. Ensure that headings and subheadings are correctly formatted and that text is aligned according to the required style guide.

- **Citation and Referencing Errors**: For academic and professional documents, accurate citations and references are essential. Verify that all sources are cited correctly and that the references follow the appropriate style guide (e.g., APA, MLA). Check for correct formatting of in-text citations and reference lists.

In summary, careful attention to spelling, grammar, punctuation, sentence structure, pronoun use, consistency, word choice, modifiers, formatting, and citations can significantly improve the clarity and professionalism of a document. By focusing on these common errors, you can enhance the quality of your writing and ensure that your message is communicated effectively.

www.ingramcontent.com/pod-product-compliance
Lightning Source LLC
Chambersburg PA
CBHW012012110726
47993CB00008B/3023